✝

Para mi hija en [?] 💙 ‖‖‖‖‖‖‖‖‖ **W9-ANU-488**

COMPANIONS FOR THE JOURNEY

de parte de: ✝

Fr. Tom Hynes, C.M.

4/21/2016

Praying with

Thérèse of Lisieux

Joseph F. Schmidt, FSC

the**WORD**
among us®
press

Copyright © 1991 by St. Mary's Press,
702 Terrace Heights, Winona, MN 55987-1320

All rights reserved

Published by The Word Among Us Press
7115 Guilford Road
Frederick, Maryland 21704
www.wau.org

18 17 16 15 14   10 11 12 13 14

ISBN: 978-1-59325-263-2

Cover design by DesignWorks Group

Cover image: © Office Central de Lisieux

No part of this publication may be reproduced, stored in a retrieval system, or transmitted in any form or by any means—electronic, mechanical, photocopy, recording, or any other, except for brief quotations in printed reviews—without the prior permission of the publisher.

Made and printed in the United States of America

Library of Congress Control Number: 2006923986

Contents

To my friends
who contributed to this book
by their encouragement, suggestions,
and love of Thérèse.

Foreword

J ust as food is required for human life, so are companions. Indeed, the word "companions" comes from two Latin words: *com*, meaning "with," and *panis*, meaning "bread." Companions nourish our heart, mind, soul, and body. They are also the people with whom we can celebrate the sharing of bread.

Perhaps the most touching stories in the Bible are about companionship: the Last Supper, the wedding feast at Cana, the sharing of the loaves and the fishes, and Jesus' breaking of bread with the disciples on the road to Emmaus. Each incident of companionship with Jesus revealed more about his mercy, love, wisdom, suffering, and hope. When Jesus went to pray in the Garden of Olives, he craved the companionship of the apostles. They let him down. But God sent the Spirit to inflame the hearts of the apostles, and they became faithful companions to Jesus and to each other.

Throughout history, other faithful companions have followed Jesus and the apostles. These saints and mystics have also taken the journey from conversion, through suffering, to resurrection. Just as they were inspired by the holy people who went before them, so too may you take them as your companions as you walk on your spiritual journey.

The Companions for the Journey series is a response to the spiritual hunger of Christians. This series makes available the rich spiritual teachings of mystics and guides whose wisdom can help us on our pilgrimages. As you complete the last meditation in each volume, it is hoped that you will feel supported, challenged, and affirmed by a soul-companion on your spiritual journey.

The spiritual hunger that has emerged over the last twenty years is a great sign of renewal in Christian life. People fill retreat programs and workshops on topics in spirituality. The demand for spiritual directors exceeds the number available. Interest in the lives and writings of saints and mystics is increasing as people search for models of whole and holy Christian life.

PRAYING WITH THÉRÈSE

Praying with Thérèse of Lisieux is more than just a book about Thérèse's spirituality. This book seeks to engage you in praying in the way that Thérèse did about issues and themes that were central to her experience. Each meditation can enlighten your understanding of her spirituality and lead you to reflect on your own experience.

The goal of *Praying with Thérèse of Lisieux* is that you will discover Thérèse's profoundly simple spirituality and integrate her spirit and wisdom into your relationship with God, with your brothers and sisters, and with your own heart and mind.

Suggestions for Praying with Thérèse

Meet Thérèse of Lisieux, a fascinating companion for your pilgrimage, by reading the introduction to this book, which begins on page 14. It provides a brief biography of Thérèse and an outline of the major themes of her spirituality.

Once you meet Thérèse, you will be ready to pray with her and to encounter God, your sisters and brothers, and yourself in new and wonderful ways. To help your prayer, here are some suggestions that have been part of the tradition of Christian spirituality:

Create a sacred space. Jesus said, "When you pray, go to your private room, shut yourself in, and so pray to your [God] who is in that secret place, and your [God] who sees all that is done in secret will reward you" (Matthew 6:6). Solitary prayer is best done in a place where you can have privacy and silence, both of which can be luxuries in the lives of busy people. If privacy and silence are not possible, create a quiet, safe place within yourself, perhaps while riding to and from work, while sitting in line at the dentist's office, or while waiting for someone. Do the best you can, knowing that a loving God is present everywhere. Whether the meditations in this book are used for solitary prayer or with a group, try to create a prayerful mood with candles, meditative music, an open Bible, or a crucifix.

Open yourself to the power of prayer. Every human experience has a religious dimension. All of life is suffused with God's presence. So remind yourself that God is present as you begin your period of prayer. Do not worry about distractions. If something keeps intruding during your prayer, spend some time talking with God about it. Be flexible because God's Spirit blows where it will.

Prayer can open your mind and widen your vision. Be open to new ways of seeing God, people, and yourself. As you open yourself to the Spirit of God, different emotions are evoked, such as sadness from tender memories, or joy from a celebration recalled. Our emotions are messages from God that can tell us much about our spiritual quest. Also, prayer strengthens our will to act. Through prayer, God can touch our will and empower us to live according to what we know is true.

Finally, many of the meditations in this book will call you to employ your memories, your imagination, and the circumstances of your life as subjects for prayer. The great mystics and saints realized that they had to use all their resources to know God better. Indeed, God speaks to us continually and touches us constantly. We must learn to listen and feel with all the means that God has given us.

Come to prayer with an open mind, heart, and will.

Preview each meditation before beginning. After you have placed yourself in God's presence, spend a few moments previewing the readings and especially the reflection activities. Several reflection activities are given in each meditation because different styles of prayer appeal to different personalities or personal needs. *Note that each meditation has more reflection activities than can be done during one prayer period. Therefore, select only one or two reflection activities each time you use a meditation. Do not feel compelled to complete all the reflection activities.*

Read meditatively. Each meditation offers you a story about Thérèse and a reading from her writings. Take your time reading. If a particular phrase touches you, stay with it. Relish its feelings, meanings, and concerns.

Use the reflections. Following the readings is a short reflection in commentary form, which is meant to give perspective to the readings. Then you are offered several ways of meditating on the readings and the theme of the prayer. You may be familiar with the different methods of meditating, but in case you are not, they are described briefly here:

- Repeated short prayer: One means of focusing your prayer is to use a "prayer word." It may be a single word or a short phrase taken from the readings or from the Scriptures. For example, the short prayer for the first meditation in this book is "I want, O my God, to love you face-to-face." Repeated slowly in harmony with your breathing, the prayer word helps you center your heart and mind on one action or attribute of God.

  🐝 *Lectio divina*: This type of meditation is "divine studying," a concentrated reflection on the word of God or the wisdom of a spiritual writer. Most often in *lectio divina*, you will be invited to read one of the passages several times and then concentrate on one or two sentences, pondering their meaning for you and their effect on you. *Lectio divina* commonly ends with formulation of a resolution.

  🐝 Guided meditation: In this type of meditation, our imagination helps us consider alternative actions and likely consequences. Our imagination helps us experience new ways of seeing God, our neighbors, ourselves, and nature. When Jesus told his followers parables and stories, he engaged their imagination. In this book, you will be invited to follow guided meditations.

One way of doing a guided meditation is to read the scene or story several times, until you know the outline and can recall it when you enter into reflection. Or before your prayer time, you may wish to record the meditation on a tape recorder. If so, remember to allow pauses for reflection between phrases and to speak with a slow, peaceful pace and

tone. Then, during prayer, when you have finished the readings and the reflection commentary, you can turn on your
recording of the meditation and be led through it. If you find
your own voice too distracting, ask a friend to make the tape
for you.

- Examen of consciousness: The reflections often will ask you
to examine how God has been speaking to you in your past
and present experience—in other words, the reflections will
ask you to examine your awareness of God's presence in your
life.

- Journal writing: Writing is a process of discovery. If you
write for any length of time, stating honestly what is on your
mind and in your heart, you will unearth much about who
you are, how you stand with your God, what deep longings
reside in your soul, and more. In some reflections, you will
be asked to write a dialog with Jesus or someone else. If
you have never used writing as a means of meditation, try
it. Reserve a special notebook for your journal writing. If
desired, you can go back to your entries at a future time for
an examen of consciousness.

- Action: Occasionally, a reflection will suggest singing a favorite hymn, going out for a walk, or undertaking some other
physical activity. Actions can be meaningful forms of prayer.

Using the Meditations for Group Prayer

If you wish to use the meditations for community prayer, these suggestions may help:

❧ Read the theme to the group. Call the community into the presence of God, using the short opening prayer. Invite one or two participants to read one or both readings. If you use both readings, observe the pause between them.

❧ The reflection commentary may be used as a reading, or it can be deleted, depending on the needs and interests of the group.

❧ Select one of the reflection activities for your group. Allow sufficient time for your group to reflect, to recite a centering prayer, to accomplish a studying prayer (*lectio divina*), or to finish an examen of consciousness. Depending on the group and the amount of available time, you may want to invite the participants to share their reflections, responses, or petitions with the group.

❧ Reading the passage from the Scriptures may serve as a summary of the meditation.

❧ If a formulated prayer or a psalm is given as a closing, it may be recited by the entire group. Or you may ask participants to offer their own prayers for the closing.

Now you are ready to begin praying with Thérèse of Lisieux, the Little Flower, a faithful and caring companion on this stage of your spiritual journey. Over the last century, Thérèse has drawn countless people to seek a closer relationship with God. We hope that you will find her to be a true soul-companion.

Introduction

Thérèse of Lisieux, commonly known as the Little Flower, died in a French convent on September 30, 1897. Her popularity rapidly extended well beyond her Carmelite convent community, her hometown of Lisieux, and her country. In 1925 Pius XI responded to the enormous outpouring of popular veneration by declaring Thérèse a saint, calling her a "Word of God" and a "master of the spiritual life" (Francois Jamart, *Complete Spiritual Doctrine of St. Thérèse of Lisieux*, trans. Walter Van De Putte, p. 7). Subsequent popes proclaimed her patroness of the missions and, with Joan of Arc, patroness of France.

The widespread veneration of Thérèse is amazing because she had no tangible achievements to her credit during the twenty-four years of her life. She did no apostolic work, founded no religious community, and engaged in no missionary activity. Except for her immediate family and her community of twenty or so Carmelite nuns, Thérèse lived virtually unknown.

A SHOWER OF ROSES

The memory of Thérèse would surely have passed from history had it not been for two phenomena immediately following her death that prompted her enormous popularity: the publication of her autobiographical writings, under the title *The Story of a Soul*, and the outpouring of miraculous assistance to hundreds of people who implored her help.

Shortly after her death, the Carmelite convent at Lisieux began receiving letters from people around the world, telling of inner healings, physical cures, spiritual illuminations, conversions, and special help received through Thérèse's intercession. The miraculous help was seen to be the "shower of roses" she had promised on her deathbed.

Thérèse's picture adorned the trenches of both German and French soldiers during World War I. Her life and spirit captured the imagination of philosophers and writers such as Henri-Louis Bergson, Paul Claudel, and Georges Bernanos. She inspired such diverse people as Dorothy Day, Thomas Merton, Mother Teresa, and Gustavo Gutierrez.

But above all, Thérèse has been the inspiration of untold numbers of ordinary people to whom her life proclaimed in a compelling way this gospel truth: God's love comes in the ordinary experiences of life, and nothing—no physical, emotional, intellectual, or spiritual weaknesses, no psychological defects or moral failures—absolutely nothing can separate us from the love of God.

THE STORY OF THÉRÈSE

Thérèse Martin was born in Alençon, France, on January 2, 1873. In the three years before Thérèse was born, the Martin family had lost four children. Consequently, Thérèse's birth was an event of great joy. Her four older sisters, Marie, Pauline, Léonie, and Céline delighted in caring for her.

Thérèse's mother, Zélie, sold lacework that she made at home, and her father, Louis, had a watchmaking business. Her mother actively managed the family; Thérèse's father was more reserved. Both parents were intelligent, reflective, and intensely religious. Prayer, popular devotions, almsgiving, conversations centering on the faith, and church attendance permeated the family's routine.

During her early childhood years, Thérèse was surrounded with an affection that affirmed and guided her. She blossomed into an expressive child: forthright, trusting, confident, sensitive, intelligent, affectionate, conscious of her own goodness and her limitations, and endowed with a sense of humor.

Thérèse's First Letter

Written on April 4, 1877, when she was four, Thérèse's first letter tells us much about her. Guided by the hand of her sister Pauline, Thérèse wrote to one of Pauline's friends:

I don't know you, but I love you very much just the same. Pauline told me to write you; she is holding me on her knees because I don't know how to hold a pen. She wants me to tell you that I'm a lazy little girl, but this isn't true because I work all day long playing tricks on my poor little sisters. So I'm a little rascal who is always laughing. Adieu, little Louise. I'm sending you a big kiss. Kiss the Visitation for me, that is, Sister Marie Aolysia and Sister Louise de Bonzague, for I don't know anyone else. (Thérèse, de Lisieux, Saint, *General Correspondence*, vol. 1, trans. John Clarke, p. 110)

But the sunny days of the first four years of childhood ended when her mother died agonizingly of breast cancer. Shocked and afflicted with profound grief, Thérèse entered a painful ten-year period during which she withdrew into herself and became overly sensitive, pensive, shy, and melancholy.

Early Years

At eight years old, Thérèse became a day student at the Benedictine Abbey school in Lisieux. Until then she had lived in the sheltered life of her family with her sister Pauline assuming the role of Thérèse's second mother. Suddenly, at the Abbey school, Thérèse was thrown into the give-and-take world of boarding-school girls. The experience proved traumatic for her. She was no longer the special one, the baby, to be showered with affection and care. For the first time in her life, Thérèse encountered rejection and ill will, becoming the object of petty jealousy.

Thérèse outshone her classmates in intelligence and academic performance but suffered self-doubt about her ability to fit in, to do things well, and to be accepted. Simply put, Thérèse did not know how to relate to her peers. In the company of her classmates, her reflectiveness and sensitivity proved to be liabilities. She became acutely aware of her limitations and incompetence and grew more introspective, not even sharing her inner distress with her father or sisters. Instead she found consolation in sharing her difficulties with Jesus, whose presence she had treasured since her earliest years.

At this point, Pauline entered the convent at Carmel. Again Thérèse suffered a maternal loss, which threw her into a distressful state of continual headaches and insomnia. Three months after Pauline's departure, Thérèse became so ill that she was bedridden with nervous trembling and hallucinations. She had suffered this emotional pain for two months, when, according to Thérèse, she saw the statue of the Virgin Mary at the foot of her bed smile at her. At that instant, she was cured.

Unfortunately, this consolation proved short lived. During her visits to Pauline at Carmel, the nuns sought to satisfy their curiosity about the smile of the statue, and their prying questions troubled Thérèse. She started wondering if she really had been all that ill, if she had actually made herself sick, and even if the smile of the Virgin was just another hallucination.

Thérèse's first Communion and the profession of her sister Pauline at Carmel brought some spiritual consolation, but within the year she entered a crisis of moral scruples and developed severe headaches. Because of her weak condition, Thérèse, now thirteen years old, was withdrawn from the Abbey school and placed with a private tutor.

In the next six months, two of her older sisters, Marie and Léonie, entered religious life: Marie at Carmel with Pauline, and Léonie with the Poor Clares. Although Thérèse found joy in the almost constant companionship of her remaining sister, Céline, four years her senior, a deep melancholy permeated her daily life, causing her to be, as she described, unbearably touchy. She prayed for inner freedom, peace, and strength against her hypersensitivity.

Thérèse's Conversion and Entrance into Carmel

God answered Thérèse's prayer through an experience that she described as a complete conversion. Just before her fourteenth birthday, on Christmas morning of 1886, Thérèse received the enlightenment and empowerment that led her into the third period of her life, a period she experienced as beautiful and filled with grace.

Thérèse had just returned home from midnight Mass with her father and Céline. Not knowing that Thérèse could overhear his words, her father impatiently commented to Céline about Thérèse's childish behavior as she opened her Christmas presents: "Well, thank goodness it's the last year this is going to happen!" (Ronald Knox, trans., *Autobiography of St. Thérèse of Lisieux*, p. 127). Such a rebuke from her father, even if unintended, pierced Thérèse's heart. But mysteriously, these words carried the miracle Thérèse had been praying for. She realized that Jesus had changed her, giving her a new inner freedom that allowed her to forget herself. Through this transforming experience, Thérèse rediscovered the strength of soul and the joy that she had lost with the death of her mother. The presence of Jesus became more vivid to her, and she gained a keener sense of her own personhood. Melancholy and touchiness left her. She became increasingly concerned for the welfare of other people.

In the May following her conversion, Thérèse requested her father's permission to enter the Carmelite convent at Lisieux. She was only fourteen years old and her father's favorite. However, her father approved and championed her cause, despite his sadness over losing his little Thérèse and distress from a minor stroke he had recently suffered.

Because Thérèse was so young, she needed the local bishop's approval to enter the convent. But when she asked for his permission, he objected that she was not old enough. Thus, only one recourse lay open. During the pilgrimage to Rome that had already been planned, Mr. Martin and Thérèse decided to seek the permission from Pope Leo XIII himself.

As the papal audience proceeded, Thérèse, ignoring all protocol, directly voiced her request to the pope. He told her to follow the directives of her superiors but reassured her, "All's well, all's well; if God wants you to enter, you will" (Knox, *Au-*

tobiography, p. 170). Then guards had to lead Thérèse out of the audience chamber.

Thérèse and her father persisted, and in the December after the papal audience, the local bishop reversed himself, granting approval for Thérèse to enter the convent at Carmel. Thus, in April 1888, at the age of fifteen, Thérèse was received into the cloister by Mother Marie de Gonzague, the superior; Pauline and Marie, her two sisters; and the twenty-three other nuns in the community.

THÉRÈSE AT CARMEL

The Community

In Carmel, Thérèse found a rhythm of life established by hundreds of years of tradition. The nuns followed the same basic schedule that Teresa of Ávila established for her community in sixteenth-century Spain.

For the youthful Thérèse it was a difficult routine. She rose at about 4:30 a.m. and, except for a brief siesta, did not rest again until 9:30 p.m. She spent six hours each day praying the Divine Office in choir and two hours in personal prayer. Her meatless meals, served at ten and six, were followed by an hour of recreation during which the nuns conversed together while sewing or doing other simple chores. For five hours every day, Thérèse did manual labor. She swept corridors, gardened, and did common tasks in the linen room, the refectory, the sacristy, or the laundry. Except for the two recreation periods, her day was spent mostly in silence and solitude.

Pauline and Marie welcomed Thérèse into the Carmelite family with great tenderness. Other nuns were more reserved, even suspicious of this fifteen-year-old. Like any group of people, the Carmelite community at Lisieux included the balanced and the eccentric, the intelligent and the slow, the joyful and the distressed. Thérèse found some of the women difficult and hurtful, others more compatible. Community life, especially her interaction with the nuns during work and recreation, challenged and nurtured Thérèse's ability to love.

Because of her conversion experience, Thérèse, who had been so withdrawn and oversensitive during the ten years following her mother's death, now became expressive and openly affectionate. Her winning personality, lost for so long, blossomed into maturity. Thérèse's capacity to accept others and be at ease even with difficult people proved to be a balm to the community. Her unassuming nature and simplicity were disarming, and her sense of humor became a source of delight. She had a gift for storytelling and good-natured mimicry.

Gradually, the older nuns began to respect Thérèse's straightforward simplicity, quiet wisdom, and profound spiritual awareness, sometimes seeking her out for spiritual advice.

Trials from the Outside
Thérèse entered Carmel to be more completely with Jesus

and to offer her life so that others, especially the priests and sinners for whom she prayed, might experience and accept God's love. Thérèse recognized that convent life would involve the suffering associated with self-knowledge, with detachment from her own self-preoccupation, with being at the service of other people, with obeying what she understood to be God's will, and with allowing her affectionate nature to be purified so that she could love others as God loves. But external sources of suffering existed as well.

One external source of great pain for Thérèse was her father's medical condition after a mild stroke. Just three months after Thérèse entered the convent, her father became so disoriented that he had to be committed to the mental hospital, where he died five years later. Even though Céline's care for their father allayed some of Thérèse's anxiety, the slow but inevitable loss of her "King," as she called him, caused Thérèse profound grief.

The regular routine and lifestyle of Carmel also caused suffering for Thérèse. Having been pampered at home, Thérèse found it difficult to adjust to the customary periods of fasting, the common work, the minimal time for rest and sleep, the lack of privacy, and the deprivation of common conveniences. The cold and damp of the seasons, against which the convent offered only a single fireplace in the recreation room, proved especially troublesome for Thérèse. The physical work, to which she was not accustomed, taxed her strength. The convent food was adequate, but Thérèse never showed preferences in what she ate. As a result, she was sometimes served the least appetizing and least nourishing dishes. Thérèse could not endure extraordinary bodily mortifications, so simply accepting life as it unfolded with all of its small irritants, inconveniences, and hurts became her form of discipline.

Inner Sufferings

In her inner life, Thérèse suffered even more intensely. In many ways, she found the spirituality at the convent too mechanical, rigorous, and filled with fear. From the day of her entrance into the cloister, Thérèse experienced an almost constant aridity or lifelessness in prayer. She could not pray or experience God in the ways most of the other nuns did. She often dozed during meditation and the times of personal prayer after Communion, and she became easily distracted while praying the Divine Office. Thérèse had come to Carmel to find Jesus, but Jesus sometimes seemed to be absent.

Only on rare occasions throughout Thérèse's nine years in Carmel did retreat directors or confessors inspire her. From her companions in Carmel she received little confirmation of her spiritual insights, and her own introspective nature did not easily move her to completely share her inner life with other people. She walked her spiritual journey almost entirely alone and frequently in inner desolation, especially as her health deteriorated.

Later, during the last eighteen months of her life, Thérèse spoke of having been invaded by "the darkness thicker than ever." She felt like she was traveling through a dark "tunnel" in a dense fog in "the night of mere nonexistence." Her sense of faith vanished, and only an impenetrable "wall which reaches right up to the sky and blots out the stars" replaced it (Knox, *Autobiography*, pp. 254, 256–257).

Sources of Strength

Throughout her spiritual journey, Thérèse took comfort in the gospels, *The Imitation of Christ*, and the writings of Teresa of Ávila and John of the Cross. When Céline also entered Carmel after their father's death, she brought some hand-copied sections of the Hebrew Scriptures to Thérèse. In many passages, Thérèse discovered confirmation of the truths that she was learning from her own experience. Proverbs 9:4, which invites little ones to God, and the reference in Isaiah 66:12-13, which describes God's maternal tenderness, were among Thérèse's favorite passages. But the Song of Songs, the psalms, and the gospels gave Thérèse her greatest joy and consolation.

Thérèse's devotional life focused both on Jesus as the divine child and Jesus as the hidden, unknown, and suffering servant spoken of in Isaiah, chapter 53, and described in the passion stories of the gospels. In the image of the child, Thérèse identified her own weakness and helplessness as well as the invitation to an unpretentious boldness and freedom in the presence of God's goodness and mercy. In the image of Jesus, the suffering servant whose holy face was hidden from recognition in life and in death, Thérèse understood the dark side of life. She came to know the power of evil and the meaning of suffering. In the image of the suffering servant, Thérèse came to identify her own call to a hidden life, a poverty of spirit, a zeal for the salvation of souls, and an acceptance of silent suffering in union with Jesus. Devotion to the suffering servant of God, under the title of the Holy Face of Jesus, was Thérèse's most important devotion.

The radiance of joy permeated Thérèse's personality and eclipsed manifestations of her physical and spiritual suffering. After her death, the nuns at Carmel were surprised to learn of her almost constant physical and spiritual trials. Through all her physical pain and spiritual desolation, Thérèse remained determined and cheerful, confident in and sustained by the belief that God dwelled with her. At a deep level in her soul she found a well of inner freedom and joy.

Thérèse as Novice Mistress

At the age of nine, while visiting Pauline, Thérèse first met Mother Marie de Gonzague, prioress at Carmel. At that time, Mother Gonzague paid Thérèse the highest compliment: she took the girl seriously, confirming Thérèse's conviction that she did have a vocation. Some weeks later, Mother Gonzague even suggested to Thérèse the name that she might choose when she would enter Carmel, the very name that had come to Thérèse in a dream that morning: Sister Thérèse of the Child Jesus. This coincidence delighted Thérèse and forged a special bond between her and the prioress.

Mother Marie de Gonzague was still prioress when Thérèse entered Carmel, and she served in this capacity for six of Thérèse's nine years in the community. While she welcomed Thérèse lovingly into the postulancy, she soon began to act with severity toward her. Mother Gonzague respected and appreciated Thérèse, but she was determined that this young girl, babied at home, would not become the pet of the community. Deeply devoted to the prioress, who was a woman of great personal vigor, Thérèse felt deep confusion and pain from the seeming rejection. But in submitting to her superior's harshness, Thérèse gradually realized and valued the discipline that helped form her. Her love for Mother Gonzague returned in a fuller, more mature way.

In 1893, five years after Thérèse entered Carmel, Mother Gonzague's term as prioress ended, and the community elected Thérèse's sister Pauline to the position. Pauline named Mother Gonzague novice directress and assigned Thérèse to be her assistant. Thus, Thérèse was put into the delicate position of working with the former prioress, who was still touchy about the election and who came to resent Pauline.

Thérèse's appointment told Mother Gonzague and the community that Pauline judged Thérèse's spiritual awareness and practice to be mature enough to form the novices. In fact, Thérèse, without offending Mother Gonzague, became the de facto novice mistress. When Mother Gonzague was re-elected prioress in another contentious election three years later, she had such confidence in Thérèse that she confirmed her in the role of assistant novice mistress.

As prioress, Mother Gonzague also remained novice mistress, choosing not to relinquish the role to the defeated Pauline, as was customary. Out of her love for both women, Thérèse mediated between them and became a confidant of Mother Gonzague. Indeed, Thérèse served as director for the five novices. She had no formal preparation for the role, and Mother Gonzague, sometimes capricious and unpredictable, gave her little useful advice. Four of the five novices were older than Thérèse, and two were relatives: her sister Céline and her cousin Marie.

Thérèse soon realized that forming novices into contemplative nuns under these circumstances was altogether beyond her, so she redoubled her prayer and relied on her own insights for guidance. With a combination of firmness and gentleness, Thérèse gained the novices' confidence and a reputation for blunt honesty, simplicity, and good judgment.

Thérèse's Illness and Death

In 1896, less than a month after Mother Gonzague had been re-elected prioress, Thérèse coughed up blood on the evening of

Holy Thursday. Her health had been deteriorating during the past months, but this was the first clear sign that Thérèse was in the early stages of tuberculosis. Thérèse reported the experience to Mother Gonzague, but with such simplicity that Mother Gonzague was not alarmed. At her own insistence, Thérèse continued to participate in the community routine, asking for no relief from the common, and now increasingly painful, daily tasks. Her health continued to fail, but a full year passed before the symptoms of the illness became so pronounced that she was forced to withdraw from community practices.

Finally she was confined to the infirmary, her health gradually ebbing away. Medical treatment for tuberculosis was largely rudimentary, and, as was customary at the time in Carmel, Thérèse was given no painkillers. Her suffering intensified with each passing day.

During the months of her illness, Thérèse continued the writing of her memoirs, a task begun earlier when Pauline, as prioress, had asked Thérèse to record her memories and some of the delightful stories of their family life. Thérèse did so sporadically over the course of a year. Then her sister Marie asked Thérèse to write reflections on her spiritual way and to share her retreat meditations. Thérèse wrote some of her thoughts during the last community retreat she made, a year prior to her death.

Now that Thérèse was clearly entering the last months of her life, Mother Gonzague directed Thérèse to finish her memoirs, especially her reflections on the years in Carmel that the earlier writings did not include. When her strength permitted, Thérèse did as she was requested, writing her story in short snatches of time.

During her struggle with tuberculosis and while finishing her memoirs, Thérèse also underwent her most severe spiritual suffering. Spiritual desolation, feelings of abandonment by God, and despair nearly overwhelmed her. Such images of terror and darkness so flooded her consciousness that she was afraid to speak of them lest she discourage her sisters or utter blasphemies. She spoke of the hissing of serpents in her ears and even of passing thoughts of suicide.

Nevertheless, Thérèse continued to believe, because, as she acknowledged, she wanted to believe. And the belief that God had led her in a way that anyone could follow provided some solace. She understood that her own life contained nothing extraordinary, and since God carried her—little and imperfect as she was—on her spiritual journey, God could bring anyone and everyone to holiness. She hoped that her prayers, writings, and the example of her brief life might bring other people to know God's love and faithfulness.

During the last two months of her life, Thérèse suffered high fevers, fits of coughing, difficulty in breathing, bed sores, and searing pain in her lungs. Medical remedies proved useless; her spiritual desolation also continued unabated. Until the end, self-doubt, frightful nightmares, spiritual darkness, and temptations to despair plagued her.

Thérèse's patience and calm smile disguised her desperate state from many of the nuns. She lingered in agony. Then on the evening of September 30, 1897, she died with her Carmelite community gathered around her and with a prayer on her lips: "Oh, I love Him! . . . My God . . . I love you!" (John Clarke, trans., *St. Thérèse of Lisieux: Her Last Conversations*, p. 206). Thérèse was twenty-four years old.

THÉRÈSE'S STORY SPREADS

Thérèse's passing would have been unmarked by the outside world except for a great number of miracles attributed to her intercession and the extraordinary history of her memoirs. Her stories of family life, reflections on her spiritual way, and recollections about her days at Carmel were combined and distributed under the title *The Story of a Soul*. The nuns at Lisieux sent the manuscript to the other Carmelite convents as a substitute for the usual obituary issued upon the death of a nun.

The nuns began lending *The Story of a Soul*, together with some of Thérèse's letters and several of her poems, to their friends and relatives. Between 1897 and 1932, 700,000 copies of these writings were distributed. Also, over two and a half million copies of a popular edition of the work were produced and sold.

Besides her memoirs, Thérèse wrote over 260 notes and letters, some poems—most composed at the request of the nuns in her community—and several plays for the edification and recreation of the nuns. Her sisters recorded Thérèse's conversations with them as they ministered to her on her deathbed during the last several months of her life. All these writings testified to a profound, simple, and inspiring holiness, all but hidden behind the walls of Carmel.

THÉRÈSE'S SPIRITUALITY

As seen from the outside, Thérèse's life was eminently simple. Those with whom she lived did not recognize her holiness. They believed that Thérèse did nothing extraordinary in her life and that the virtue she manifested came quite naturally to her. When Mother Gonzague heard that the cause for Thérèse's canonization might be introduced in Rome, she remarked that if such were the case, then many of the nuns would be eligible.

Thérèse composed no theories of spiritual life and preached no great sermons before throngs of believers. Rather, her spirituality flowed from her little experiences. Indeed, her spirituality became known as the "Little Way," which has the following characteristics:

God Loves Each of Us

François Jamart wrote that in her life and her understanding of love, Thérèse proclaimed this fundamental gospel message: "God is merciful Love, a love that stoops down in order to draw us to Himself. 'The proper characteristic of love,' she wrote, 'is that it stoops down . . . it must stoop down even to nothingness and transform that nothingness into fire.' It was Thérèse's mission to teach us 'a way of confidence and love,' . . . She called this 'the way of spiritual childhood'" (Jamart, *Complete Spiritual Doctrine*, p. 7).

God Is the Source of Our Love

Thérèse rejoiced in the awareness that God acts most powerfully by stooping down in mercy. God, like a loving parent, delights in helping the weak and struggling child. God loves us first and is the source of our love and goodness. Then, we can become channels of God's own love.

Trust in Providence

By faithfully responding to the daily experiences that Divine Providence offered her, Thérèse expressed her desire to please God. She did not have the capacity, as she readily admitted, to be a great saint, but she was confident that God wished her to be a saint. Unable to be like the giant trees in the forest, she would give God delight by being a piece of moss or a little flower on the forest floor. She would not be discouraged by her own inadequacies or weaknesses, but would give God the pleasure of her complete surrender to his mercy.

Poverty of Spirit

By giving special attention and love to the little, the simple, the weak, and the poor parts of life and of herself, Thérèse showed us how to live in poverty of spirit. Her life testified to the truth that the little ones, those who are poor in spirit, are special to God, are in touch with truth, and contribute to the building up of the church. Thérèse reminds us that many little saints fill the church, even though we may not recognize them in their simple garb and plain ways. These are the people who accept their own limitations and weaknesses, and open themselves to God in total trust. These little saints receive God's love and mercy and allow that love to flow through them to others by responding to what they believe God wills.

One source of Thérèse's poverty of spirit was the sharp sense she had of her own weaknesses. By weakness, she meant not only her failings, human limitations, and inner conflicts, but also her capacity to stray from the path of personal authenticity, truth, and inner freedom. She recognized that she was capable of rejecting God's will for her and of compromising her own identity and call. She lived with her weaknesses, confident that God's grace would give her strength.

Love for Other People

Thérèse had an affectionate nature, nurtured by the love of her family. Community life in Carmel brought her face-to-face with her own antipathies and taught her to care for other people despite these adverse feelings. Love for other people meant fostering and doing freely, without compulsion, the best good for them in the circumstances in which she found herself. As Thérèse matured she learned to respond in love, not because she felt compelled by her desire to please, but because she saw the good in other people and could empathize with their difficulties, having accepted her own inadequacies and weaknesses. *Dgh*

Search for Truth

From her youngest days, Thérèse offered her heart to God as a daily morning prayer. To be heart-to-heart with God became the theme of Thérèse's life and the way she expressed her desire to be totally authentic with God. She sought to unmask her personal illusions and dishonesty and to open herself to the spirit of truth. Through her prayer, reflection, and in her writing, Thérèse made seeking the truth of her life with God a lifelong quest.

THÉRÈSE FOR TODAY

Thérèse is the saint of the "Little Way," the way of spiritual childhood. She characterized her way as being like a little child who is lifted up by God through the daily events of life. With eyes ever on God, the child responds to that love, knowing that God's mercy transforms all. As she reflected on her life, Thérèse recognized that God led her, with all her inadequacies and littleness, to holiness. She assures us that God can do the same for us.

In 1997 Pope John Paul II conferred on Thérèse the title "Doctor of the Universal Church," an honor she now shares with only thirty-two other saints. "Her Doctrine," the pope proclaimed in his apostolic letter *Divini Amoris Scientia*, "is at once a confession of the Church's faith, an experience of the Christian mystery, and a way to holiness. Thérèse offers a mature synthesis of Christian spirituality." Thus Thérèse's message is not limited to some special school of spirituality; nor is it only of passing interest. Thérèse is a saint for all of us in these modern times.

MEDITATION ONE
Heart-to-Heart with Jesus

Theme: At the core of Thérèse's spirituality was her awareness of Jesus' invitation to intimacy with him in which heart speaks to heart.

Opening prayer: "I want, O my Beloved, at each beat of my heart to renew my offering to You an infinite number of times, until the shadows having disappeared I may be able to tell You of my Love in an Eternal Face to Face!" (John Clarke, trans., *Story of a Soul: The Autobiography of St. Thérèse of Lisieux*, p. 277)

ABOUT THÉRÈSE

Thérèse developed a deep affection for all the members of her family, but especially for her father. His pet name for his youngest daughter was "my little Queen," and Thérèse returned the affection by calling him the "King." Often they would speak heart-to-heart. Thérèse described the scene when, at fourteen, she opened her heart to her king, requesting his permission that she might enter the Carmelite convent:

I chose Pentecost as the date for making my disclosure.
. . . I found the opportunity of speaking to him, this

well-loved father of mine. He had gone outside and was sitting by the well, the wonderful book of nature spread out before him. . . . On his handsome face there was an expression of heavenly calm, and you could see that his soul was utterly at peace. I went up and sat there beside him without saying a single word, but my eyes were wet with tears. He looked down at me ever so tenderly, and pressed my head close to his heart: "What's the matter, little princess?" he said. "Tell me about it." Then he got up, as if to disguise his own feelings, and began to walk up and down, still holding me close to his side.

When I told him about my longing to enter Carmel, his tears came out to meet mine, but he didn't say a word to discourage my vocation. He only suggested that I was still very young to take such a serious resolution. But I put up such a good case for myself that Papa, with his honest, straightforward nature, was quick to see the will of God in these promptings of mine; and so deep was his faith that he cried out: "What an honour God is doing me, in asking me like this for the gift of one daughter after another!" Our walk didn't come to an end all at once; my heart went out to his, in gratitude for the kindness with which he'd received my confidences. What a wonderful father to have! He seemed now to be experiencing the calm and happiness which are the reward of making a sacrifice. It was like talking to a Saint; how I wish that I could recall his words and put them on paper! But it is all a faint memory, laid up in lavender; . . . I'll only mention one thing which stands out in my memory—an action of his which was symbolic, though it wasn't meant to be.

There were some little white flowers, rather like lilies, growing on a low wall close by. He picked one of these flowers and gave it to me, pointing out how it was God's care that had fostered this plant and kept it in being. As I listened to him, I felt I was listening to the story of my own life; so close was the analogy between them, the insignificant flower and the insignificant Thérèse! (Knox, *Autobiography*, pp. 139–140)

Experiences such as this with her father and family nurtured Thérèse's capacity to share heart-to-heart with God. Years later Thérèse wrote to her sister Céline: "I speak to Him then in the solitude of this delightful heart-to-heart, while waiting to contemplate Him one day face-to-face . . . " (Thérèse de Lisieux, Saint, *General Correspondence*, vol. 2, trans. John Clarke, p. 709).

Pause: Ponder Thérèse's image of being heart-to-heart with Jesus.

THÉRÈSE'S WORDS

About a year before her death, Thérèse wrote to her sister Léonie:

I assure you that God is much better than you believe. He is content with a glance, a sigh of love . . . As for me, I find perfection very easy to practice because I have understood it is a matter of taking hold of Jesus by His heart.

. . . Look at a little child who has just annoyed his mother by flying into a temper or by disobeying her. If he hides away in a corner in a sulky mood and if he cries in fear of being punished, his mamma will not pardon him, certainly, not his fault. But if he comes to her, holding out his little arms, smiling, and saying: "Kiss me, I will not do it again," will his mother be able not to press him to her heart tenderly and forget his childish mischief? . . . However, she knows her dear little one will do it again on the next occasion, but this does not matter; if he takes her again by her heart, he will not be punished. (*General Correspondence*, vol. 2, pp. 965–966)

As she lay suffering on her deathbed, Thérèse summed up her lifelong attitude of being heart-to-heart with Jesus and wishing to please God:

If God were to say to me: If you die right now, you will have very great glory; if you die at eighty, your glory will not be as great, but it will please Me much more. I wouldn't hesitate to answer: "My God, I want to die at eighty, for I'm not seeking my own glory but simply Your pleasure."

The great saints worked for the glory of God, but I'm only a little soul; I work simply for His pleasure. . . . (Clarke, *Her Last Conversations*, p. 102)

REFLECTION

The custom of pouring out her passionate heart to Jesus, a practice common from her childhood, became an essential part of Thérèse's spirituality. The images of lying on the heart of Jesus, taking Jesus by the heart, or being the playmate of Jesus became foundational images for Thérèse.

Taking Jesus "by his heart" expresses tender intimacy and total confidence in Jesus. It is an image of receiving God's compassionate love, of pleasing God, and of responding to God's love. Thérèse understood that "taking hold of Jesus by his heart," not the formal fulfillment of rules, comprised genuine perfection and holiness.

❧ Read the section "About Thérèse" slowly again. Let yourself visualize each part of the scene. How do you feel about her father's way of dealing with Thérèse? How has God cared for you just as God cared for the Little Flower?

🌺 Given the great love showered upon her by her mother and father, Thérèse firmly believed that God was like a loving parent, always prepared to pardon. But sometimes, the thought of our sinfulness may inhibit us from being heart-to-heart with God.

Are there some areas of sinfulness in your life that you find hard to share with God, heart-to-heart? Ponder an experience that you find difficult to share with God; be aware of the feelings the memory evokes. Tell God as much as you can about the experience, especially about the distress that comes to you as you remember it. Pray for the grace to embrace God's love for you, to accept yourself, and to be more open in your relationship with God.

🌺 Allow Thérèse's image of God as a loving parent, welcoming you and tenderly caring for you, to fill your imagination. Spend time with this image.

- What are your feelings in the presence of such a caring God?

- What would you wish to say to God, and what would God reply to you?

❧ Reflect on your childhood years and remember one special occasion when you felt the care and affection of someone. Allow that memory to unfold in detail. Recall the place, the specifics of what you as a child did and said, and what the caring person did and said. Offer a prayer for the person who shared that love. If the person is still living and can be contacted, consider thanking him or her in some way in the next several days or weeks.

❧ Be quiet within yourself and be aware of God's presence. Be attentive to your breathing, and in rhythm with your breathing, recite this prayer of thanksgiving. As you inhale, pray slowly, "I want, O my God"; and as you exhale, "to love you face-to-face." Pray this way for four or five minutes.

❧ Imagine yourself resting on God's heart. Express to God what is in your heart.

❧ Reflect on Thérèse's belief that she worked for God's pleasure. In what ways does that thought challenge you in your relationship with God? Let thoughts and images come to you as you reflect on what it would mean for you to live and work only for God's pleasure.

FROM GOD'S WORD

You will be suckled, carried on her hip
and fondled in her lap.
As a mother comforts a child,
so I shall comfort you; . . .
(Isaiah 66:12-13, NJB)

Closing prayer: Oh, Jesus, "I do not want to lay up merits for heaven. I want to work for Your Love alone with the one purpose of pleasing You, consoling Your Sacred Heart." (Clarke, *Story of a Soul*, p. 277)

Loving in Response to God's Protective Love

Theme: With full knowledge of her own weakness and limitations, Thérèse held fast to God's protective love that not only forgives faults but actually prevents us from falling.

Opening prayer: Oh God, "if your Justice, which finds its scope on earth, demands to take its course, how much stronger must be the impetus which impels your merciful love to take possession of souls! Your mercy . . . reaches up to heaven itself." (Knox, *Autobiography*, p. 220)

ABOUT THÉRÈSE

In a remarkable way Thérèse's childhood was filled with love. Her parents and older sisters acted lovingly toward one another and treated her with profound and generous affection. However, Thérèse also experienced misunderstanding, inner conflict, and personal limitations. As a child she was corrected for her faults forthrightly.

When, at age eight, Thérèse entered the school of the Benedictine nuns in Lisieux and began to interact with other children, she came face-to-face with her inadequacies. She remarked, "I did not know how to play like the other children, and I was not much fun for them, but I did do my best to join in, even though it was never any good" (Ida Friederike Görres, *The Hidden Face: A Study of St. Thérèse of Lisieux*, p. 67).

As a Carmelite nun, Thérèse came to know her weaknesses with more clarity, and she identified with no one more than with Mary Magdalene. From Magdalene, Thérèse learned that God's love comes first, protecting and sustaining us, forgiving us, and inviting our love in response:

> It was only God's mercy that preserved me . . . ; without that, I might have fallen as low as St. Mary Magdalen did. . . . I owe him more than the Magdalen herself; he remitted my sins beforehand, as it were, by not letting me fall into them. Oh dear, I wish I could explain exactly what I feel about it. Put it like this—a clever doctor has a son who trips over a stone, falls, and breaks a limb. His father is at his side in a moment, picks him up tenderly, and treats his injuries with all the skill he has. Thanks to him, the boy is completely cured before long; and the father, sure enough, has done something to earn his love. But now, suppose the father sees the stone in his son's path, runs ahead of him and takes it out of the way,

without calling any attention to what he is doing. At the time, the boy is unconscious of the danger he would have run, but for his father's foresight; is less grateful, less moved to affection, than if a cure had been performed. But if he learns afterwards what risks he has been spared, the boy will love him more than ever. And that's what God's loving providence has done for me. When he sent his Son into the world, it was to ransom sinners, not the just—yes, but, you see, in my case he has left me in debt to him not for much but for everything. He hasn't waited to make me love him much, like the Magdalen; he's made me realise what I owe to his tender foresight, to make me love him to distraction, as I do. (Knox, *Autobiography*, pp. 113–114)

Pause: When you look back, can you think of times when God took care of you in a difficult situation without your being aware of it or even when you thought that God had forgotten you?

THÉRÈSE'S WORDS

Along with the realization of her weakness and belief in God's protecting love, Thérèse knew that God would illumine her path and give her ample grace to respond to God's call. God loved and protected her first; now she was called to be protective love for other people:

In consideration of my weakness, you found a way to
fulfil my childhood's ambitions, and you've found a way
now to fulfil these other ambitions of mine, world-wide in
their compass.

I was still being tormented by this question of unful-
filled longings and it was a distraction in my prayer, when
I decided to consult St. Paul's epistles in the hopes of getting an answer. It was the twelfth and thirteenth chapters
of First Corinthians that claimed my attention. The first
of these told me that we can't all of us be apostles, all of
us be prophets, all of us doctors, and so on; the Church is
composed of members which differ in their use; the eye is
one thing and the hand is another. It was a clear enough
answer, but it didn't satisfy my aspirations, didn't set my
heart at rest. . . . Reading on to the end of the chapter, I
met this comforting phrase: "Prize the best gifts of heaven.
Meanwhile, I can shew you a way which is better than
any other."

What was it? The Apostle goes on to explain that all
the gifts of heaven, even the most perfect of them, without love, are absolutely nothing; charity is the best way of
all, because it leads straight to God. Now I was at peace;
. . . charity—that was the key to my vocation. . . . Love
was the true motive force which enabled the other members
of the Church to act; if it ceased to function the Apostles
would forget to preach the gospel, the Martyrs would refuse

to shed their blood. Love, in fact, is the vocation which includes all others. . . . Beside myself with joy, I cried out: "Jesus, my Love! I've found my vocation, and my vocation is love." (Knox, *Autobiography*, pp. 234–235)

REFLECTION

Thérèse was thrice blessed in her youth: in knowing that she was loved from the beginning, in realizing her limitations and weaknesses, and in being aware that the two experiences were mysteriously compatible. Even in her early years, Thérèse acknowledged this fundamental gospel truth: only in our weakness does God's powerful love find a home. Throughout her life Thérèse was graced with experiences from which she learned that because she was weak, little, and fallible, God would protect her out of love for her. As a result, she could truly love God and others because she was flooded with God's love. Toward the end of her life, when she spoke of finding her vocation to love, she again identified herself with Mary Magdalene, who, although she was weak and had faults, was loved and loved others in return.

❧ Read the section "Thérèse's Words" again. When a phrase strikes you, read it again slowly, several times. Ponder and cherish its meanings for you.

☙ Thérèse experienced God's loving her with "tender fore-sight" that prevented her from falling. Reflect on some of the significant events of each phase of your life, times when you could have easily gone in the wrong direction or fallen into compulsions or vice. Then ask yourself how God's providence cared for you in each event of these phases:

- young adulthood

- adolescence

- childhood

- infancy

Thank God for loving providence in the past and constant pro-tecting love now and in the future.

☙ It is a truth-telling paradox that only when we experience our own personal failings and weaknesses do most of us realize that God's powerful love protects us from harm. Experiences in childhood often acquaint us with our personal limitations.

Find a photograph of yourself as a child, or picture your-self as a child in your imagination. Look into the eyes of the child and imagine the child's feelings at that time in regard to your weaknesses and limitations. Now recall an experience occurring about that time in your life that made you feel bad, powerless, or imperfect. Allow the memories of the incident to linger. Then speak to God about the experience, sharing with God any pain in the memory. Imagine how much God loved you at that childhood moment, and allow the Spirit to comfort you now.

❧ Reflect on an aspect of your life in which you presently experience moral weaknesses or compulsion—an aspect of your life for which you need the forgiveness of God and of your neighbor.

First consider what need that weakness or compulsion might be filling, what security or compensation it might be giving you. Pray that, if it is God's will, you may cease needing that weakness and that God might be your sole security.

Then ask for God's forgiveness for this failing and for assistance in overcoming it. Pray also that God's love will abound in that area of your life and that you may be led to a deeper love and compassion for other people.

❧ The Christian vocation, or call, is to love God and to love our neighbor as ourself. In some practical ways, how could you show God's protective love by smoothing the way in advance for someone else or by taking action for the good of other people, even before they might ask? For instance, parents show God's preventive love by keeping dangerous objects out of children's reach. People participate in God's protective love by recycling and living simply—all in an attempt to protect God's creation for future generations. How are you being called to be God's protective love?

FROM GOD'S WORD

Though I command languages both human and angelic—if I speak without love, I am not more than a gong or a cymbal clashing. And though I have the power of prophecy, to penetrate all mysteries and knowledge, and though I have all the faith necessary to move mountains—if I am without love, I am nothing. Though I should give away to the poor all that I possess, and even give up my body to be burned—if I am without love, it will do me no good whatever. . . .

As it is, these remain: faith, hope and love, the three of them; and the greatest of them is love. (1 Corinthians 13:1-3, 13, NJB)

Closing prayer: "Oh, I know quite well that I am only a child, with all a child's weaknesses; but that's precisely what emboldens me to offer myself as a victim to your love. . . . Love cannot be content without condescending—condescending to mere nothingness, and making this nothingness the fuel for its flame." (Knox, *Autobiography*, pp. 235–236)

MEDITATION THREE
Inner Freedom

Theme: God calls each of us to our unique conversion, desiring that we be free from inner compulsions that hinder our ability to love.

Opening prayer:
>   "To You alone, O Jesus, I must cling;
>   and running to Your arms, dear Lord,
>   There let me hide;
>   Loving with childlike tenderness."
>   (Thérèse, in Jamart, *Complete Spiritual Doctrine*, p. 88)

ABOUT THÉRÈSE

By the time Thérèse approached her teen years, she believed that her happiness was dependent on her ability to please. Thérèse summed up her sense of being in bondage to her feelings when, referring to her older sister, she said, "If poor Céline omitted to look happy and surprised about these good deeds of mine, I was miserable about it and burst into tears." Thérèse was more concerned with calming her own sensitivities and pleasing others than with being true to herself. She knew that

"God had to perform a miracle on a small scale to make me grow up" (Knox, *Autobiography*, p. 126).

That little miracle was granted to Thérèse on Christmas morning, just days before her fourteenth birthday. That morning she received

the grace to leave my childhood's days behind; call it, if you will, the grace of complete conversion. We'd just got back from Midnight Mass. . . . I would go off to find my Christmas slipper in the chimney corner; we'd loved this so much in our childhood that Céline went on treating me as if I were a baby, as being the youngest. Papa was always so fond of seeing my happiness, and listening to my cries of delight as the magic slipper revealed, one after another, my surprise presents, and part of my enjoyment was the pleasure he took in it. But this time, our Lord meant to shew me that I ought to be getting rid of my childish defects; so this innocent joy was denied me, and he allowed Papa to be the means of my disappointment. He, Papa, was tired after the Midnight Mass, and the sight of my slippers in the chimney corner annoyed him. Imagine my distress when I overheard him saying: "Well, thank goodness it's the last year this is going to happen."

I was going upstairs at the moment, to take off my hat; Céline, who knew how touchy I was, saw my eyes shining with tears and was ready to cry herself; in her loving sympathy, she knew exactly what I was feeling. . . . But she didn't know the Thérèse she was dealing with; our Lord had changed me into a different person. I dried my tears and went down at once; my heart was beating fast, but I managed to get hold of my slippers and put them down in front of Papa, and as I took out my presents you would have thought that I was as happy as a queen. Papa smiled, his good humour restored, and Céline thought she must be dreaming. But no, it was a sublime reality; baby Thérèse had recovered the strength of mind which she'd lost at four and a half and recovered it for good. (Knox, *Autobiography*, pp. 127–128)

That Christmas Thérèse received the grace of being aware of her compelling need for the affirmation of others. Her father's chance remark became the means to her enlightenment. Thérèse recognized that her conversion to inner freedom was a pure gift. It was a breakthrough into a new capacity to forget the need for approving responses and to love others. She said of herself, "Charity had found its way into my heart" (Knox, *Autobiography*, p. 128).

Throughout her life, Thérèse remained prone to spontaneously trying to please other people, but she was also a woman of integrity and courage. Both her desire to please and her inner freedom manifested themselves as she lay on her deathbed. One of the sisters noted,

We had made preparations for her to receive Holy Communion the next day. . . . Seeing that she was sicker than usual, we feared she would cough up blood after midnight, and so we asked her to pray that no such unfortunate incident take place to interfere with our plans. She answered:

"I . . . [asked] God for this favor in order to please my little sisters and so that the community might not be disappointed; but in my heart I told Him just the contrary; I told Him to do just what He wanted." (Clarke, *Her Last Conversations*, pp. 98–99)

Pause: Reflect on the need you may have for the approval of others and consider whether that need limits your inner freedom.

THÉRÈSE'S WORDS

Four years after her conversion, at the age of seventeen, Thérèse wrote this prayer for her profession of vows in Carmel:

Jesus, my heavenly Bridegroom, never may I lose this second robe of baptismal innocence; take me to yourself before I commit any wilful fault, however slight. May I look for nothing and find nothing but you and you only; may creatures mean nothing to me, nor I to them—you, Jesus, are to be everything to me. May earthly things have no power to disturb the peace of my soul; that peace is all I ask of you, except love; love that is as infinite as you are, love that has no eyes for myself, but for you, Jesus, only for you. Jesus, I would like to die a martyr for your sake, a martyr in soul or in body; better still, in both. Give me the grace to keep my vows in their entirety; make me understand what is expected of one who is your bride. Let me never be a burden to the community, never claim anybody's attention. . . . May your will be perfectly accomplished in me, till I reach the place you have gone to prepare for me. (Knox, *Autobiography*, pp. 201–202)

REFLECTION

We may be quite aware of our lack of freedom because of restrictions other people place on us or because of our own limitations. However, we may not be aware of our lack of freedom when we become trapped by our own feelings. The grace of Thérèse's Christmas conversion showed her that she could be aware of her feelings and yet not be overwhelmed by them, thus retaining her inner freedom. God's grace brought Thérèse to conversion; she turned from her old ways and toward the liberating God.

To all of us, God extends an invitation to inner freedom. We may need to turn from the oppression of anger, greed, shame, or fear. Each of us has some chain holding us back from surrendering ourselves to God's love. But, as in the case of Thérèse, God calls us and provides abundant grace for a change of heart, mind, and will—for conversion.

❧ Read again slowly and meditatively the section "Thérèse's Words." If a line strikes you as particularly significant, stay with it. Let Thérèse's wisdom touch you.

❧ Consider a recent incident in which you experienced difficult and upsetting feelings. They may be feelings of anger or hurt, fear or guilt, or just distress and confusion. Recall the incident for a few minutes and write a short description of what happened.

Allow your mind to drift to a time of your childhood when those same feelings were present. Recall and write about the circumstances surrounding that childhood experience. Notice what was happening at that time of childhood and write down what you as a child might have said at that time about that experience. And now, what would you as an adult say to that little child? Share some comfort with the child.

Finally, speak with God about that childhood experience. Allow God to express care and healing for you in that experience. /

❧ Bring to mind a person whose approval is very important to you. You may or may not like the person. In memory and imagination, reconstruct a situation during which you experienced the need for this person's approval, as well as the hurt and fear associated with not having it. Share with God what it would mean for you not to need that person's approval any longer. Ask God to help you take possession of that area of your heart and allow that area to be filled with God's approval.

❧ Consider an incident in the recent past when you may have disregarded what you knew God wanted of you in order to please someone. Pray with Thérèse that even as you please others when you can, you will always have the freedom in your heart to allow God's will to be fulfilled.

❧ God called Thérèse to conversion through what seemed to be a chance remark by her father. Perhaps you have been deeply affected by an offhand remark, either positively or negatively. Recall such an experience. What was said, and what did you feel? Was there any element of truth in the comment? Pray that God will allow you to accept whatever you know to be true, no matter who it comes from.

❧ List the aspects of your life that most easily turn your attention away from God. From what attachments, compulsions, or sinful ways do you need conversion? Open yourself to God's grace for conversion by naming each chain that keeps you from God, and then pray like Thérèse: "Jesus, may your will be perfectly accomplished in me, till I reach the place you have gone to prepare for me." Use this prayer when you need to turn back to God's way.

FROM GOD'S WORD

It is no longer I, but Christ living in me. (Galatians 2:20, NJB)

Closing prayer: O God, "May I look for nothing and find nothing but you and you only; . . . May earthly things have no power to disturb the peace of my soul." (Knox, *Autobiography*, p. 202)

MEDITATION FOUR

Loving with God's Love

Theme: Thérèse experienced God's love as "waves of infinite tenderness" flooding her and all creation (Clarke, *Story of a Soul*, p. 277). In yielding herself to God's love, she boldly loved God and other people with God's love.

Opening prayer:

"You, the great God, whom all heaven adores,
you live in me, a prisoner night and day;
the whole time your gentle voice implores me,
you keep on saying, "I am thirsty . . . I thirst for love."
I also am your prisoner,
and I want to say back to you
your own tender and divine prayer,
'My beloved, my brother, I thirst for love.' "
(Thérèse, untitled poem, in Simon Tugwell, *Ways of Imperfection: An Exploration of Christian Spirituality*, pp. 224–225)

ABOUT THÉRÈSE

Over the years, Thérèse confidently began to expect everything from God. Her oldest sister, Pauline, said of Thérèse, "Her

---

loving confidence in our Lord made her extraordinarily daring in the things she asked him for. When she thought of his all-powerful love, she had no doubts about anything" (Christopher O'Mahony, ed. and trans., *St. Thérèse of Lisieux by Those Who Knew Her*, p. 46).

Thérèse knew that her love for God and for other people was not her love at all, but rather God's love flowing through her:

> Dear Lord, you never tell us to do what is impossible, and yet you can see more clearly than I do how weak and imperfect I am; if, then, you tell me to love my sisters as you love them, that must mean that you yourself go on loving them in and through me—you know it wouldn't be possible in any other way. There would have been no new commandment, if you hadn't meant to give me the grace to keep it; how I welcome it, then, as proof that your will is to love, in and through me, all the people you tell me to love!
>
> Always, when I act as charity bids, I have this feeling that it is Jesus who is acting in me; the closer my union with him, the greater my love for all the sisters without distinction. What do I do when I want this love to grow stronger in me? How do I react, when the devil tries to fix my mind's eye on the defects of some sister who hasn't much attraction for me? I remind myself, in a great hurry, of all that sister's good qualities, all her good intentions. True enough, she's made a slip this time; but who's go-

ing to tell us how often she's fought temptation and conquered it, only she was too humble to let us notice it?

It's even possible that what I think of as a fault was in reality a praiseworthy act—it depends on the intention. (Knox, *Autobiography*, p. 266)

Pause: Do you, like Thérèse, believe that when you love someone, it is really God's love flowing through you?

THÉRÈSE'S WORDS

A few months before she died, Thérèse boldly prayed,

Dear Jesus, I don't know how long it will be before my banishment comes to an end; there may be many evenings yet that will find me telling the tale of your mercies, still in exile. But for me, too, there will be a last evening; and then, my God, I would like to be able to offer to you the same prayer. "I have exalted thy glory on earth, by achieving the task which thou gavest me to do. . . . This, Father, is my desire, that all those whom thou hast entrusted to me may be with me where I am, and that the world may know that thou hast bestowed thy love upon them, as thou hast bestowed it upon me. . . ."

My God, you know that the only thing I've ever wanted is to love you; I have no ambition for any other glory except that. In my childhood, your love was there waiting for me; as I grew up, it grew with me; and now it is like a great chasm whose depths are past sounding. Love breeds love; and mine, Jesus, for you, keeps on thrusting out towards you, as if to fill up that chasm which your love has made— but it's no good; mine is something less than a drop of dew lost in the ocean. Love you as you love me? The only way to do that is to come to you for the loan of your own love; I couldn't content myself with less. Dear Jesus, I can have no certainty about this, but I don't see how you could squander more love on a human soul than you have on mine! That's why I venture to ask that these souls you've entrusted to me may experience your love as I have. . . . (Knox, *Autobiography*, pp. 307–309)

REFLECTION

Thérèse understood that true love is not the result of personal achievement, but of complete availability to God, so that care, compassionate service, and affection are God's love flowing through us.

🌢 Reflect on a specific, recent event through which you experienced God's love. In what way were you especially blessed by God's love? Thank God for the love you were shown.

Call to mind a particular person in your life whom you would ask God to bless in the same way. Pray that God will bless this person.

&. Other people mediate God's love to us, too. Consider all the people who have shown you charity, friendship, and nurturing love. If possible, find pictures of these loving people. Recollect how each person has shown you love, and then thank God for sending each one into your life.

&. Thérèse had confidence in God's loving providence, not in anything she herself had done. On her deathbed, Thérèse prayed that she would fly to "the Sun of Love on the eagle-wings you, and you only, can lend me."

If the sun is shining, go and walk in its warmth. If you cannot go out or if the day is cloudy or dark, close your eyes and imagine a glorious sunny day. Consider all the ways in which we depend on the sun. Then ask yourself: How much more do I depend on God's free gift of love than I do on the sun?

Next, allow the vision of being borne to God on the wings of God's own love to fill your imagination. In what ways does this image of being borne by God's love and not your own accomplishments console you? In what ways does it challenge you?

&. Sometimes we find particular people hard to love. Think of a person who is so bothersome that you feel you cannot love him or her. Remember a particular occasion when you were disturbed or distressed by this person. Share with God the difficulties you had relating to this person. Pray that you can be more accepting of yourself and less fearful, angry, or self-deprecating in this person's company.

Imagine Jesus accepting and caring for this person. Pray that you might be aware of God's love for this person and that God's love for this person will flow through you. Then ask God to enlighten you about what inside you prevents you from loving him or her. Ask God to free you of the things that block your ability to love.

❧ Pray a litany of thanks for the times when you have felt God's love flowing through you to other people. For instance, you might compose your litany like this: "For letting me console Alex yesterday at the funeral of his father, I thank you, Sun of Love."

❧ Thérèse took the words of the father of the prodigal son to be words of God addressed to herself: "All I have is yours." Pray these words slowly, over and over, knowing that God speaks them to you. Then, talk with God about what you most need to be fully alive, fully able to love.

FROM GOD'S WORD

"All I have is yours." (Luke 15:31, NJB)

Closing prayer: O Jesus, "I am too poor a creature to do anything wonderful, but I must be allowed the folly of hoping that . . . these eagles of yours, my elder brothers, . . . win me the grace I need, that of flying upwards towards the Sun of Love on the eagle-wings you, and you only, can lend me" (Knox, *Autobiography*, p. 241).

MEDITATION FIVE

The flowering of Little Sacrifices

Theme: For Thérèse, sacrifice took the form of being aware of her own willfulness and then yielding it to God's will, even in small matters.

Opening prayer:
"Jesus, my only Love, at the feet of your Calvary
how I love to scatter flowers each evening!
In plucking the petals of the springtime rose for you
I would like to dry your tears. . . .
To scatter flowers is to offer as first fruits the slightest sighs,
the greatest sufferings,
my sorrows and my joys, my little sacrifices.
These are my flowers."
(Thérèse, in Redemptus Valabek, "Thérèse's Approach
to Gospel Living," in John Sullivan, ed., *Experiencing St.
Thérèse Today*, p. 77)

ABOUT THÉRÈSE

When Thérèse spoke of loving God, she immediately thought of proving that love in practice. But she knew that she would never perform great or notable works for God; little sacrifices had to suffice in proving her love. Like a rose that blooms and then drops its petals, she would simply lose herself to give God pleasure. To be completely at the disposal of God, she would allow the vicissitudes of life to free her of all attachments. Accepting sacrifices would be the flowers she would scatter before God's throne.

Thérèse's great capacity was in loving, and her sacrifices were the result of loving. Unlike many of the saints, and indeed many of her contemporaries, Thérèse was not attracted to doing penance. She explained her views on sacrifice and mortification this way:

> When I say "mortified," I don't mean to suggest that I went in for penitential practices of any kind. That's a thing, I'm afraid, I've never done. . . . What I did try to do by way of mortification was to thwart my self-will, which always seemed determined to get its own way; to repress the rejoinder which sometimes came to my lips; to do little acts of kindness without attaching any importance to them. . . . (Knox, *Autobiography*, p. 181)

Each small sacrifice helped Thérèse detach herself from her self-centered desires and feelings. To be special in the eyes of others, to have her own way, to have beautiful things around, to want spiritual consolation and peacefulness at prayer, to have the validation of her feelings and the acknowledgment of her gifts, were ordinary, sometimes trivial desires, but they were thoughts and preferences Thérèse would give up. She stood confident that God's care would be enough.

Toward the end of her life, Thérèse acknowledged that she experienced some of her greatest difficulties in freeing herself from her attachment to the interior gifts:

There are certain movements of the mind and the heart, certain deep-reaching thoughts, that go to form a treasury of your very own; nobody else, you feel, has a right to tamper with it. For instance, I tell one of the sisters, when we have leave to talk, about some light that has been given to me in prayer; and she, quite soon afterwards, mentions it to a third party in conversation as if it were an idea of her own; isn't that pilfering? Or again, in recreation, I whisper some remark to the person next [to] me, a good remark, absolutely to the point; and she repeats it aloud without mentioning where it came from; isn't that theft of my property? I can't say so at the time, but I'd like to; and if opportunity arises, I determine to let it be known, with all the delicacy in the world, that somebody's been misappropriating my thoughts.

If I can describe them so exactly, Mother, these deplorable instincts of our nature, it is because I have felt them in my own heart. . . . I really think I can say, now, that our Lord's given me the grace to care as little about gifts of the mind and the heart as about worldly possessions. (Knox, *Autobiography*, pp. 277–278)

Pause: What little services have you rendered today without the desire for recognition?

THÉRÈSE'S WORDS

But this love of mine, how to shew it? Love needs to be proved by action. Well, even a little child can scatter flowers, to scent the throne-room with their fragrance; even a little child can sing, in its shrill treble, the great canticle of Love. That shall be my life, to scatter flowers—to miss no single opportunity of making some small sacrifice, here by a smiling look, there by a kindly word, always doing the tiniest things right, and doing it for love. (Knox, *Autobiography*, p. 237)

The largest and most beautiful flowers of sacrifice that Thérèse gave in love were those she culled from the garden of her relationships.

One significant sacrifice that Thérèse had to make was her powerful affection for Mother Gonzague, the prioress of Carmel. Mother Gonzague's authority, charm, and vitality so captivated Thérèse that she feared she might lose her focus on God. Later, Thérèse wrote to Mother Gonzague:

How well I remember the violent temptations I had, when I was a postulant, to make my way into your room, just for the pleasure it gave me; a crumb of comfort now and again! I had to pass the business-room at full speed, and cling tight to the banisters. Couldn't I go and ask leave to do this and that? Such thoughts crowded into my mind; I can't tell you, Mother, what a lot of excuses occurred to me for getting my own way. And how grateful I am now that I kept myself in hand during those early days! There's a reward promised to people who fight bravely, and I'm glad to say I've got it already. . . . I find, to my great delight, that when you love [God] the capacities of your heart are enlarged, so that your feelings towards those who are dear to you are infinitely more tender than they would have been, if you had devoted yourself to a selfish kind of love which remains barren. (Knox, *Autobiography*, p. 283)

Thérèse believed that by detaching herself from her need for Mother Gonzague's attention and care she would be free to accept God's love, which would flow to her in abundance. Thérèse draws this conclusion about "little sacrifices":

The food of real love is sacrifice; just in proportion as you deny yourself any kind of self-indulgence, your affection for the other person becomes something stronger, and less self-regarding. (Knox, *Autobiography*, pp. 282–283)

Reflection

For Thérèse the spirit of detachment grew as an expression of love. She wanted to be completely available to God and not mired in her own sentimentality and self-centeredness. While she was aware of the subtle bondage into which any attachments could lead her, at the core of Thérèse's stance of detachment was her willingness to refuse God nothing and never to fail in an opportunity to prove her love for Jesus.

The good news challenges all Christians to place God's will first. Loving God and our neighbor frequently demands small, but sometimes large, sacrifices of our own desires.

❧ At one point, Thérèse compares inordinate emotional attachments to the affection a dog has for its master (Knox, *Autobiography*, p. 282). Allow that image to come alive in your imagination. Are you in relationship with any person or thing to which that image could be applied? Share with Jesus your feelings about that relationship or any relationship in which you feel too attached and unfree.

❧ Sometimes the sacrifices asked of us flow from unchangeable circumstances in our life. These unchangeable demands may provoke resentment, and we often have no sense of "scattering flowers" for Jesus.

List some of the demands of ordinary life that you cannot change and that provoke anxiety, resentment, or depression. Then, next to each demand, list ways in which it could become an opportunity to sacrifice some of your ignorance, pettiness, self-centeredness, impatience, and so on. How could you turn the demand into flowers strewn at the feet of Jesus?

Finally, ask God to show you ways to give up your destructive desires and feelings in unchangeable circumstances. Pray the Serenity Prayer: "God grant me serenity to accept the things I cannot change, courage to change the things I can, and wisdom to know the difference."

❧ Thérèse performed her little sacrifices of love in a way that went unnoticed even by those who lived closely with her. Recall a time when you had feelings of hurt or anger because you did not receive recognition for some good that you did or some sacrifice that you made.

- Do you need to be noticed, praised, or respected by others for your actions?

- What does the recognition of others do for you?

Pray for those from whom, especially as a child, you expected but did not receive attention, praise, or respect. Ask God to bless that child in you, and to bless you now as an adult. Pray that your relationship with God might begin to fill that area of need.

❧ Recall as many instances as you can of little sacrifices that you made for love of family, friends, co-workers, and other people. Thank God for each of these sacrifices and for the chance to build the reign of God, even if only in small ways.

From God's Word

All that we suffer in the present time is nothing in comparison with the glory which is destined to be disclosed for us. (Romans 8:18, NJB)

Closing prayer: O loving God, help me to know in my own life that "true love is found only in complete self-forgetfulness, and it is only after we have detached ourselves from every creature that we find Jesus." (Jamart, *Complete Spiritual Doctrine*, p. 119)

MEDITATION SIX

Loving Beyond Family Affection

Theme: Within her family, Thérèse learned to love. She came to understand that since God loved everyone, God called her to love everyone, too.

Opening prayer: "What is going to open my heart wide? Nothing but love. Once the heart has been melted down in this gentle flame, what a pleasure it is, dear Jesus, to run along this new path . . . [till] I shall be able to follow you with a new song; what song will it be? It can only be the song of love." (Knox, *Autobiography*, p. 272)

ABOUT THÉRÈSE

Thérèse's affectionate nature, nurtured in the sheltered world of her family, could have remained closed to new relationships. Even when she entered Carmel, Thérèse joined two of her sisters, Pauline and Marie. Later another of her sisters, Céline, and a first cousin, Marie, entered the convent, too. Living with so many of her relatives, Thérèse easily could have given into the temptation, as her sisters partly did, of trying to form a private family within the cloister. This possibility caused some concern in the small convent.

However, the nuns of Carmel came to notice that Thérèse's love included all of them. This caused some hurt and jealousy to her blood sisters. Christopher O'Mahony observes that her sister Marie once complained,

"I was a mother to her and yet you'd think she loved that sister whom I can't stand better than she does me." At recreation [Thérèse] never went out of her way to meet her own three sisters. She chatted with any nun, no matter who she was, and especially with anyone she felt was lonely or left out. (O'Mahony, *Those Who Knew Her*, p. 51)

One of the nuns who was not naturally inclined to like Thérèse noted,

"I did not have many personal dealings with Sister Thérèse. I must even have appeared quite indifferent to her. And yet, in our infrequent meetings I felt the warmth of her affection for me and a charity that flowed from her ardent love of God and her deep humility." (O'Mahony, *Those Who Knew Her*, p. 279)

Sister Teresa of Saint Augustine, the nun for whom Thérèse had the least natural affection, told of a brief conversation she had with Thérèse. She said to Thérèse,

"I'm not asking you to join us for a while; you have your own sisters, so you must have very little free time."

"Oh, don't think that," [Thérèse] said, "I don't spend any more time with them than I do with the rest: you are all my sisters." (O'Mahony, *Those Who Knew Her*, p. 194)

Pause: Ponder how you are called to love beyond the limits of your feelings of affection.

THÉRÈSE'S WORDS

About a year before she died, Thérèse wrote,

During this last year, dear Mother, God has been very gracious to me in making me understand what is meant by charity. Well, of course, I did understand it before, but only in a very imperfect way; I hadn't got to the bottom of what Jesus meant when he said that the second commandment is like the first, "Thou shalt love thy neighbor as thyself." I was making a special effort to love God better; and in doing that, it was borne in upon me that it was no use as long as my love simply expressed itself in words. . . . At the Last Supper [Jesus] makes it clearer still. . . . He says to [the Apostles]—oh, so tenderly!— "I have a new commandment to give you, that you are to love one another; that your love for one another is to be like that love I have borne you. The mark by which all men will know you for my disciples will be the love you bear one another."

Well, how did Jesus love his disciples? And why did he love his disciples? You may be quite sure that their natural qualities did nothing to attract him. . . . They were only poor sinners, so ignorant, their thoughts so earthbound; and yet Jesus calls them his friends, his brothers. He wants them to reign with him in his Father's kingdom; he is determined to win them admission, even if it means dying on a cross. . . .

Meditating on these words of Jesus, Mother, I began to see how imperfect my own love was; it was so obvious that I didn't love my sisters as God loves them. I realise, now, that perfect love means putting up with other people's shortcomings, feeling no surprise at their weaknesses, finding encouragement even in the slightest evidence of good qualities in them. But the point which came home to me most of all was that it was no good leaving charity locked up in the depths of your heart. "A lamp," Jesus says, "is not lighted to be put away under a bushel measure; it is put on the lamp-stand, to give light to all the people of the house." The lamp, I suppose, stands for charity; and the cheerful light it gives isn't meant simply for the people we are fond of; it is meant for everybody in the house, without exception. (Knox, *Autobiography*, pp. 264–265)

REFLECTION

Toward the end of her life, Thérèse realized more fully that her response to the first commandment, to love God, was to be expressed in the second commandment, to love all her neighbors. Jesus called Thérèse, and he calls us, to love all people—whether attractive or not, worthy or not, responsive or not. God gave Thérèse, and he gives us, the grace to love everyone.

🙏 Slowly read the section "Thérèse's Words" again. If a phrase touches you in some way, give it additional attention, letting its special significance become apparent. Then meditate on these questions:

- Does Thérèse's understanding of charity differ from mine?

- Do I assume that I can love only those whom I like or those who are faultless?

- Do I find that I love people more if they have more appealing qualities?

Converse with Jesus about your answers to these questions.

🙏 Thérèse knew that her capacity to love others would develop as she became freer from expectations about herself and others.

Think of a troublesome relationship that you have with a family member or co-worker.

- What do I feel when I consider this person?

- Are those distressful feelings coming from my disappointed needs in the relationship?

- Would my ability to love this person increase if I had fewer expectations of her or him?

- While respecting myself and any personal responsibilities I have in the relationship, what expectations can I appropriately give up regarding this person? *↑↓*

- Can I abide some of the person's weaknesses and faults, and forgo some of my disappointed needs relative to this person?

- How can I reduce my expectations of myself and this person?

- Is there anything I can do now in my relationship with this person as a result of these considerations?

Commend this person to God's love, and ask God to help you to love him or her as God does.

❧ Many loving experiences nourished Thérèse's deep natural affection for her family. Unfortunately, many people have not been so blessed. If you have distressful memories about your family, or feelings of fear, hurt, or anger in regard to certain family members, you may wish to continue this meditation. Writing your reflections may prove especially helpful. The loving God, who knows all things, is with you.

Recall your earliest distressful family memory. In your imagination, recreate that childhood scene. Recall the setting, the people involved, and what happened. Be especially aware of the thoughts and feelings that you had.

Next, invite Jesus into the scene. Let your child-self speak to Jesus about the experience. Then listen to Jesus' response: What would Jesus say to your hurt child-self? In your imagination, allow Jesus and your child-self to continue the dialog until the child has said all that it wants to say and has been comforted. ╰─

Now return to the present. Talk with Jesus, the healer, about how that painful childhood experience may still be affecting you. Ask God to bless you with continued healing of that past experience and those difficult feelings. Also, ask God to bless each of the family members involved in the painful experience.

🍂 If you have a photograph of your family, spend some time looking at each person. If none is available, let your mind picture each of your family members. Invite your memories and feelings about each member to come to you. As you remember each one, speak to God about how you relate to that person. Give thanks for each person, ask forgiveness for any harm that you have brought, and request God's help for each of you.

🍂 Examine the ways in which you share your gifts, talents, skills, and resources with people who are hungry, ill, imprisoned, uneducated, homeless, or needy in some other way. If you need to share more fully with needy people, determine a course of service.

🍂 Pray repeatedly the sentiments "From God's Word."

FROM GOD'S WORD

His mother and his brothers came looking for him, but they could not get to him because of the crowd. He was told, "Your mother and brothers are standing outside and want to see you." But he said in answer, "My mother and my brothers are those who hear the word of God and put it into practice." (Luke 8:19-21, NJB)

Closing prayer: Gracious Jesus, "There would have been no new commandment, if you hadn't meant to give me the grace to keep it; how I welcome it, then, as proof that your will is to love, in and through me, all the people you tell me to love!" (Knox, *Autobiography*, p. 266).

MEDITATION SEVEN
Holding Fast and Giving Way

Theme: Thérèse could act with uncompromising firmness or with sensitive accommodation once she determined how God wanted her to love.

Opening prayer: I pray with Thérèse, "Jesus, for love of you, I've poured out my life, my future." (Valabek, "Approach to Gospel Living," in Sullivan, *Experiencing St. Thérèse*, p. 81)

ABOUT THÉRÈSE

As years passed, Thérèse learned that she did not have to impose her own preferences on others, because she did not have to protect or prove herself. She had the ability to accept and appreciate herself, but not the need to indulge in self-pity or self-seeking. She was free to stand firm or give in to other people, whichever love called for.

Thérèse possessed a natural firmness of character. Her effort to enter Carmel at age fourteen testifies to this strength of purpose. Once she had decided that God was calling her, she went with her father to the bishop and personally requested the prelate's permission. She received no definite approval. So a few weeks later, while on pilgrimage to Rome, she took further steps. During a papal audience, she disregarded the directives of the papal assistants that allowed no one to speak to the pope and boldly addressed Leo XIII himself. After the pope responded, "Very well, my child, do what your superiors tell you," Thérèse countered simply, "Yes, but if you'd say the word, Most Holy Father, everybody would agree." Two papal guards had to carry her away by force (Knox, *Autobiography*, pp. 169–170).

Uncompromising in fulfilling what she believed was God's will, Thérèse was equally unflinching in accommodating herself to the tastes and whims of others when she could do this with integrity, peace, and joy. Thérèse told this story about herself:

For a long time, at evening prayers, my place was just in front of a sister who had an odd nervous affection . . . . The moment she came in she began to make a curious little noise, rather like what one would make by rubbing two shells together. Nobody noticed it except me; but then I've got a very sensitive ear—perhaps too sensitive on some occasions. I simply can't describe to you, Mother, how that tiny noise got me down. I longed to turn round and give the offender one look; obviously she was quite unconscious of fidgeting, and it didn't seem as if there was any other way to let her know about it. But something told me—something deep down inside me—that the right thing to do was to put up with it for love of God, and spare the sister any embarrassment. So I stayed still, and tried to get closer to God; perhaps I could forget it altogether, this tiny noise. . . . Absolutely useless; there was I with the sweat pouring down me, in the attempt to make my prayer into a prayer of mere suffering! Suffering—but somehow I must get rid of the nervous irritation, and suffer peaceably, joyously; that is, with peace and joy deep down in my soul. So I hit on the idea of trying to like this exasperating noise, instead of trying vainly not to hear it. I devoted myself to listening hard, as if the sound were that of some delightful music, and all my prayer—it certainly wasn't the prayer of quiet!—consisted in offering this music to our Lord. (Knox, *Autobiography*, pp. 298–299)

Pause: Consider the thoughts and feelings that prevent you from accommodating others in arbitrary matters that go against your own preferences.

THÉRÈSE'S WORDS

When Thérèse became the de facto novice mistress, she experienced both the need to be firm and the need to occasionally accommodate the novices for their own spiritual good. Love demanded strength of purpose and gentle flexibility. In responding to both needs, she put her natural tendency to please others at the service of what she believed to be God's preference:

[While working with the novices,] what takes it out of me most is having to mark down every fault in them, even the slightest imperfection, and declare war on it. . . . I would so much rather be blamed myself than have to find fault with other people! But I realise it's a good thing that it should go against the grain with me. . . .

Of course, they think I'm terribly strict with them, these lambs of your flock. If they read what I'm writing now, they would say: "That's all very well, but she doesn't seem to mind it much, running about after us and lecturing us." . . . Never mind; let them say what they will, at the bottom of their hearts, they know that I really do love them; . . . but my love for them is on such a rarefied level that they're not allowed to feel it. Never, by God's grace, have I made any attempt to engage their affection for myself; I know well enough that my business is to bring them to God. . . .

The novices, Mother, as you're aware, are quite free to tell me exactly what they think, pleasant or unpleasant, without the least restraint. That comes easy to them, because they don't feel bound to treat me with respect, as if I were a real Novice-mistress. . . . God lifts the veil that hides my imperfections, and these dear young sisters of mine see me just as I am; they don't care for that very much. They tell me, with delightful frankness, all about the rough time I give them, and my unpleasant habits, with so little embarrassment that you would imagine they were talking about somebody else. (Knox, *Autobiography*, pp. 284–285, 291–292)

REFLECTION

When she believed that God's preference required it, Thérèse's naturally strong will served her well. She was not intimidated by the criticism of others or by her own sensitivity, as her dealings with the novices point out. Nor was she cowed by the dignity of others or her feelings of fear, as shown in her interaction with the pope.

In her firmness toward the novices, Thérèse experienced some pain of rejection and others' displeasure. But rather than feeling inadequate or uneasy, she delighted in the novices' honesty and freedom, and she was free, honest, and secure enough to respond in their best interest.

In accommodating the sister in choir, Thérèse was not hostile, nor did she act in denial or without integrity. She was fully aware of her weariness caused by the noise, but she also understood that God's preference was that she remain calm and noncritical, uniting herself with God in peace and joy.

Thérèse models the way in which Christians must balance

assertiveness and flexibility, determined courage and accommodation, all at the service of love, which is the whole law of Christ and God's ultimate will for us.

𝆕 Think of a recent situation in which you allowed your preferences to be disregarded. Allow that situation to unfold in your memory and recall as best you can your thoughts and feelings at that time.

- Did you allow your preferences to be disregarded out of a sense of inner weakness, a fear of displeasing others, or a fear of not fulfilling your own or others' expectations? Or did you act out of inner strength and a conviction that the other person must have freedom too?

- Did you accommodate because you were fearful or because you were free and aware that some greater good needed to be advanced?

Allow your memory to play on that experience and share your feelings with God. Pray for deeper self-awareness. Pray for yourself and the others involved.

𝆕 Remember a recent event in which you were assertive and did not allow your preferences to be disregarded.

- Did you act on your preferences out of a sense of freedom, an inner strength, and an awareness that some larger good needed to be advanced? Or were you assertive out of hurt, anger, or a need to dominate?

- Did you demand your preferences with a sense of truth and peace?

Share with God your feelings surrounding that experience, and pray for yourself and the others involved.

❧ Recall a recent incident when you did not allow your preferences to be disregarded, but afterwards experienced some sense of distress and guilt. Pray about that incident; ask God's enlightenment to know more clearly your motivation in that incident, and to know when you need to hold fast or to give way.

❧ With whom in your life can you be more accommodating without compromising truth and peace? Who needs your sensitivity? Allow a prayer for yourself and others to flow from your considerations.

❧ With whom in your life do you need to be more firm and assertive as an expression of truth and peace? Who needs your uncompromising firmness? Let your prayer for yourself and others come from your reflections around this issue.

FROM GOD'S WORD

[Jesus said:] "Give to everyone who asks you, and do not ask for your property back from someone who takes it." (Luke 6:30, NJB)

Closing prayer: "[O] Divine little Brother, My only joy on this earth is to be able to make you happy." (Thérèse, in "Approach to Gospel Living," in Sullivan, *Experiencing St. Thérèse*, p. 73)

MEDITATION EIGHT

The Hidden Way of Spiritual Glory

Theme: We are all called to holiness. For Thérèse holiness consisted of the hidden way of love in complete trust and abandonment.

Opening prayer: O God, "let us love our littleness, . . . then we shall be poor in spirit, and Jesus will come to look for us, and however far we may be, He will transform us in flames of love." (*General Correspondence*, vol. 2, p. 999)

ABOUT THÉRÈSE

Most of Thérèse's contemporaries understood holiness to consist of eradicating faults, developing heroic virtues, enduring severe sacrifices, and achieving a level of spiritual excellence. Thérèse saw that holiness was God's doing: "Perfection appears easy, and I see that it is enough to acknowledge our nothingness, and like children surrender ourselves in the arms of God" (Görres, *The Hidden Face*, p. 337).

At about the age of twelve, Thérèse read accounts of the marvelous deeds of great heroines such as Joan of Arc. As a result, she wrote,

How I longed to imitate them; how strong it seemed to beat in me, this heroic ardour of theirs, this sense of divine inspiration! And it was in that connexion that a great grace came to me; the greatest, I always think, I have ever received in my life. . . . God put into my mind that ideal which I've just mentioned. The glory which was reserved for me was one which didn't reveal itself to human eyes; I must devote myself to becoming a great saint. That sounds conceited, of course, when you consider how imperfect a creature I was and still am. . . . But this daring ambition of aspiring to great sanctity has never left me. I don't rely on my own merits, because I haven't any: I put all my confidence in him who is virtue, who is holiness itself. My feeble efforts are all he wants; he can lift me up to his side and, by clothing me with his own boundless merits, make a saint of me. I didn't realize, then, how much suffering it had got to cost, this road to sanctity; but God lost no time in assuring me of that, by sending me the trials. . . . (Knox, *Autobiography*, pp. 97–98)

Thérèse understood that holiness would be God's achievement, not hers, and that she could be like a child in God's arms. She also acknowledged that her holiness would both be hidden and involve suffering. This understanding attracted Thérèse to the image of the child lifted up by God and to the image of the hidden, suffering Jesus: "Our Lord hadn't wanted any kingdom in this world, and he shewed me that 'if you want to learn an art worth knowing, you must set out to be unknown, and to count for nothing': . . . If only my face could be hidden away, like his, . . . that was all I longed for" (Knox, *Autobiography*, p. 188). ⌢ ⌄

Thérèse proclaimed her devotion to both the divine Child and the forgotten and suffering Jesus in a special way when she chose Sister Thérèse of the Child Jesus and the Holy Face for her religious name. Her sister Pauline reported that Thérèse's devotion to the Holy Face, through which she identified with Jesus, suffering and unknown, became the fundamental devotion of Thérèse's spirituality and one that sustained her throughout the sufferings of her life.

Pause: Have you ever been brought closer to God during a time of suffering by having complete confidence in God's providence?

THÉRÈSE'S WORDS

Several months before she died, Thérèse wrote,

As you know, dear Mother, I've always wished that I could be a saint. But whenever I compared myself to the Saints there was always this unfortunate difference— they were like great mountains, hiding their heads in the clouds, and I was only an insignificant grain of sand, trodden down by all who passed by. However, I wasn't going to be discouraged; I said to myself: "God wouldn't inspire us with ambitions that can't be realised. Obviously there's nothing great to be made of me, so it must be possible for me to aspire to sanctity in spite of my insignificance. I've got to take myself just as I am, with all my imperfections; but somehow I shall have to find out a little way, all of my own, which will be a direct shortcut to heaven. . . . Can't I find a lift which will take me up to Jesus, since I'm not big enough to climb the steep stairway of perfection?" So I looked in the Bible for some hint about the lift I wanted, and I came across the passage where Eternal Wisdom says: "Is anyone simple as a little child? Then let him come to me." To that Wisdom I went; it seemed as if I was on the right track; what did God undertake to do for the childlike soul that responded to his invitation? I read on, and this is what I found: "I will console you like a mother caressing her son; you shall be like children carried at the breast, fondled on a mother's lap." Never were words so touching: never was such music to rejoice the heart—I could, after all, be lifted up to heaven, in the arms of Jesus! And if that was to happen, there was no need for me to grow bigger; on the contrary, I must be as small as ever, smaller than ever. (Knox, *Autobiography*, pp. 248–249)

When Thérèse was on her deathbed, her sister Pauline asked her to explain what she meant by "remaining a little child before God." Thérèse replied,

It is to recognize our nothingness, to expect everything from God as a little child expects everything from its father; it is to be disquieted about nothing, . . . having no other occupation but to gather . . . the flowers of love and sacrifice, and of offering them to God in order to please Him.

To be little is not attributing to oneself the virtues that one practices, believing oneself capable of anything, but to recognize that God places this treasure in the hands of His little child to be used when necessary; but it remains always God's treasure. Finally, it is not to become discouraged over one's faults, for children fall often, but they are too little to hurt themselves very much. (Clarke, *Her Last Conversations*, pp. 138–139)

REFLECTION

Thérèse's way of holiness emphasized total confidence in God's powerful love, especially in the face of her weakness and faults. But her way was hardly naive or sentimental, because she also emphasized the need to accept, in hiddenness and trust, the suffering that purified her. Thérèse's devotion to the infancy of Jesus allowed her to express a sense of freedom, joy, and confidence, while her devotion to the passion of Jesus enabled her to embrace suffering, pain, and the dark side of life. Thérèse was sure that she would be led to holiness through her loving response to God in the ordinary experiences of life. *TJH (Ch. 15)*

❧ Slowly read the section "Thérèse's Words" and meditate on its meaning. Then consider these questions:

- In what way is the passage consoling to you?

- In what ways does it call you to have deeper confidence in God?

❧ Thérèse desired to be a saint and was convinced that God could not inspire desires in us that are not realizable. Pray with these questions:

- Do you believe that you are called to holiness?

- Have you ever desired to be a saint or to be holy? *yes*

- If so, what did being a saint or being holy mean to you at the time? In what ways has your notion of holiness changed since then?

- Did you assume that sanctity was up to you and acquired by your efforts? *yes*

- Is anything stopping you from being carried like a little child to the bosom of God? *No*

- Do you want to work your way to heaven or can you trust God to draw you along?

- How can you let go and let God sustain and direct you? Ask God to bring you to the sanctity God wishes. *Amen.*

❧ Thérèse offers two images for holiness: being held in the loving arms of God and being raised up in the arms of Jesus. Let one or both of those images fill your mind. Relax your body and close your eyes. Imagine yourself being held in God's arms or being raised up in the arms of Jesus.

Share what is in your heart with God or with Jesus.

❧ Thérèse understood that to live with integrity and to respond to God's will often entails suffering. Thérèse endured both physical and spiritual pain but still spread joy among the sisters because of her confidence in God's will. Reflect on the suffering in your life:

- At the present time, what are some ways in which you are suffering because of trying to love, be faithful, and live with integrity?

- Do you suffer any chronic physical and/or emotional pain? If so, how do you cope with this pain? Does anything prevent you from relieving some of the pain by changing what you can? How can you peacefully accept the pain that you cannot relieve?

Pray that you may accept the grace to peacefully and joyfully enter into God's design for you.

❧ For several minutes, pray slowly and repeatedly these words: "Surrender ourselves in the arms of God."

❧ Meditate on the passage from Isaiah 40:11 below. Memorize the passage and pray with it during spare moments in your day.

FROM GOD'S WORD

Like a good shepherd feeds the flock,
So God, our shepherd, feeds us.
We are gathered in his arms,
and carried next to his bosom.
God leads us with tender care.
(Adapted from Isaiah 40:11)

Closing prayer: "Dear Jesus, how I wish I could explain to all the souls that are conscious of their own littleness, how great your condescension is! I am certain that if, by some impossible chance, you could find a soul more feeble, more insignificant than mine, you could overwhelm it with graces still more extraordinary, provided that it would give itself up in entire confidence to your infinite mercy. . . . I implore you to look down in mercy on a whole multitude of souls that share my littleness; to choose out for yourself a whole legion of victims, so little as to be worthy of your love." (Knox, *Autobiography*, pp. 241–242)

MEDITATION NINE

Praying the Way You Can

Theme: Thérèse never became proficient in the usual techniques of prayer. Instead she simply prayed the way she could.

Opening prayer: "I understand, Jesus, the most captivating beauty: your divine look has penetrated my heart. All my gifts are really so few. It's my soul itself that I ought to offer you, my loving Savior." (John Russell, "The Religious Plays of St. Thérèse of Lisieux," in Sullivan, *Experiencing St. Thérèse*, p. 50)

ABOUT THÉRÈSE

As a child Thérèse learned to pray in her own way. Her father took her fishing, and Thérèse remembered that while he fished, "I even tried fishing too, with a small rod of my own; but I preferred sitting there on the grass, with the flowers for my company. . . . Although I knew nothing about meditating, my soul did sink into a state of genuine prayer" (Knox, *Autobiography*, p. 60).

Thérèse bypassed techniques of prayer. Rather, she said that when she prayed, "I tell God what I want quite simply, . . . and he always manages to understand me."

As a nun she frequently felt little consolation in prayer. So she offered herself to Jesus as his little playtoy, like a child's ball, that Jesus could use as he wished. She pictured Jesus letting his toy fall to the ground as he went off to sleep.

During formal prayers Thérèse often fell asleep. Even during her retreats, Thérèse failed to find much consolation in times of prayer:

> I ought really to have said something about the retreat I made before my profession; it brought no consolation with it, only complete dryness and almost a sense of dereliction. Once more, our Lord was asleep on the boat; how few souls there are that let him have his sleep out! He can't be always doing all the work, responding to all the calls made upon him; so for my own part I am content to leave him undisturbed. I dare say he won't make his presence felt till I start out on the great retreat of eternity; I don't complain of that, I want it to happen. It shews, of course, that there's nothing of the saint about me; I suppose I ought to put down this dryness in prayer to my own fault, my own lukewarmness and want of fidelity. What excuse have I, after seven years in religion, for going through all of my prayers and my thanksgivings as mechanically as if I, too, were asleep? But I don't regret it; I think of little children lying asleep, under the loving eyes of their parents; I think of the surgeons who put their patients under an anaesthetic—in a word, I remem-

ber how God knows the stuff of which we are made, and can't forget that we are only dust. . . . I always have the feeling that our Lord doesn't supply me with provisions for my journey—he just gives me food unexpectedly when and as I need it; I find it there without knowing how it got there. It simply comes to this, that our Lord dwells unseen in the depths of my miserable soul, and so works upon me by grace that I can always find out what he wants me to do at this particular moment. (Knox, *Autobiography*, pp. 198–199)

Pause: Consider that God nourishes you spiritually at each moment in ways that you do not know.

THÉRÈSE'S WORDS

What an extraordinary thing it is, the efficiency of prayer! Like a queen, it has access at all times to the Royal presence, and can get whatever it asks for. And it's a mistake to imagine that your prayer won't be answered unless you've something out of a book, some splendid formula of words, specially devised to meet this emergency. If that were true, I'm afraid I should be in a terribly bad position. You see, I recite the Divine Office, with a great sense of unworthiness, but apart from that I can't face the strain of hunting about in books for these splendid prayers—it makes my head spin. There are such a lot of them, each more splendid than the last; how am I to recite them all, or to choose between them? I just do what children have to do before they've learnt to read; I tell God what I want quite simply, without any splendid turns of phrase, and somehow he always manages to understand me. For me, prayer means launching out of the heart towards God; it means lifting up one's eyes, quite simply, to heaven, a cry of grateful love, from the crest of joy or the trough of despair; it's a vast, supernatural force which opens out my heart, and binds me close to Jesus. (Knox, *Autobiography*, p. 289)

In her final weeks of life, as she lay in agony, Thérèse spoke with her sisters about prayer:

". . . I can no longer pray. I can only look at the Blessed Virgin and say, 'Jesus!' . . . I can't sleep, I'm suffering too much, so I am praying."

"And what," [her sister Céline asked] "are you saying to Jesus?"

"I say nothing to Him, I love him." (Clarke, *Her Last Conversations*, pp. 224, 228)

REFLECTION

In her writings, Thérèse often mentioned the unique way Jesus leads each soul. She remained confident that Jesus was leading her in prayer even though she never became proficient at prayer forms.

Thérèse's way of praying grew intuitively from her great desire to love God. She knew what lovers know: the desire to love is love, and the desire to be totally available to God is prayer. Her desire to pray led her instinctively, even if that way was not the way she or others expected.

Prayer could be "lifting up one's eyes, quite simply, to heaven," or "a cry of grateful love, from the crest of joy or the trough of despair." Thérèse prayed in her own way, not comparing herself with other people and not being concerned about their expectations.

❦ Review the last several months and recall an occasion when, although not following any particular method of prayer, you experienced yourself sharing concerns with God. Note in detail what was happening within you. Thank God for the Spirit's action on that occasion and for the continual presence of the Spirit in your life.

❦ Recall a time when you felt that prayer was especially important to you. It may have been a single incident or a more prolonged period lasting several days or weeks. Reflect on what form your prayer took at that time: What was the place and occasion of the prayer? What did you pray about? What were the sentiments and characteristics of the prayer? Let the experience of that prayer return to you. Thank God for the gift of prayer at that time in whatever form it took.

❧ Take some time to ponder your present circumstances of living and working. Share with God, as honestly as you can, what is in your life and in your heart. Speak plainly with God about your present experiences.

❧ Do you consider the insights and awareness you receive during your daily occupations as inspirations from God? Do you experience the creative energy to initiate what needs to be done as coming from the Holy Spirit?

Plan a specific time during the remainder of this day, or tomorrow, when you will be able to pause and be consciously aware of any inspirations God might be offering. Try to foresee when you will especially need God's assistance. Pray now that you will be aware of God's presence and love at that time.

❧ Thérèse acknowledged that many times her prayer was dry; she even says that she noticed that she prayed "mechanically as if I, too, were asleep." Yet she continued to take the time to pray. She knew that children are still loved by their parents when the children are asleep; and that surgeons actually put their patients under an anaesthetic. Thérèse had a wonderful way of understanding God's mercy and tenderness. Reflect on Thérèse's truth that "God knows the stuff of which we are made, and can't forget that we are only dust," and pray that the experience of God's tenderness and mercy will fill your heart and remove all fear and any personal regret. Pray also that everyone will come to know God's tenderness and mercy.

᠅ Let your prayer be simply the desire to love Jesus more completely. In a quiet rhythm with your breathing, recite slowly and repeatedly the name of Jesus.

᠅ When she was desolate, Thérèse slowly recited an Our Father or a Hail Mary. Join Thérèse in reciting those prayers.

FROM GOD'S WORD

Yahweh is merciful and forgiving,
slow to anger, rich in love;
As tenderly as a father treats his children,
so Yahweh has compassion on those who fear him.
Yahweh knows what we are made of;
Yahweh remembers that we are dust.
(Adapted from Psalm 103: 8,13-14)

Closing prayer: O God, with Thérèse, I pray now by simply saying to you what I wish to say, knowing that you will understand me; and I want to say . . .

Being Pleasant and Gracious

Theme: Nowhere does Thérèse's inner strength and freedom emerge in fuller bloom than in her ability to be pleasant and gracious in the face of her own feelings of antipathy.

Opening prayer: "Jesus, my heavenly Bridegroom, . . . may earthly things have no power to disturb the peace of my soul; that peace is all I ask of you, except love; love that is as infinite as you are, love that has no eyes for myself, but for you, Jesus, only for you." (Knox, *Autobiography*, pp. 201–202)

ABOUT THÉRÈSE

Graciousness and pleasantness have been identified with Thérèse so much that it is sometimes assumed that her genuine goodness consisted simply of sentimental and pious sweetness. Thérèse was, indeed, a pleasant and cheerful person, but her life was not always pleasant. Cheerfulness and kindness did not come easily. Some of the nuns in Carmel disliked Thérèse and did not hide the fact; others acted thoughtlessly or insensitively toward her. Their behavior hurt Thérèse, and she admitted that she was sometimes filled with antipathy toward several of the nuns. In return, Thérèse did not act harshly, bitterly, or rudely, but she did acknowledge that being pleasant and acting kindly cost her very much.

Thérèse described what it cost her to offer one sister her "best smile":

> I can remember one act of charity God inspired me to do while I was still a novice; . . . I used to kneel just behind [Sister St. Peter] at evening prayers, and I knew that at ten minutes to six trouble was coming to somebody, because she had got to be piloted into the refectory, . . . it cost me something to make the offer, because I knew poor Sister St. Peter wasn't easy to please; she was very ill, and didn't like having a change of guides. But it seemed too good an opportunity to be missed; what did our Lord say about charity? He told us that if we did anything for the most insignificant of his brethren, we should be doing it for him. . . . Every evening, the moment I saw Sister St. Peter shaking her hour-glass at me, I knew that meant: "Let's go."
>
> You wouldn't believe how much I minded being disturbed in this way, at first anyhow. But I lost no time in making a start, and we had to make a real ceremony of it. I had to move the bench and carry it away just so, without any sign of hurry—that was important—and then the procession began. The thing was to walk behind the poor invalid holding her up by her girdle; I did this as gently

as I could manage, but if by some piece of bad luck she stumbled, she was down on me at once—I wasn't holding her properly, and she might easily fall: "Heavens, girl, you're going too fast; I shall do myself an injury." Then, if I tried to walk still slower, it was: "Here, why aren't you keeping up with me? Where's your hand? I can't feel it, you must have let go. I shall fall, I know I shall. How right I was when I told them you were too young to look after me!"

We would get to the refectory at last, without accidents. There were more obstacles to be got over; Sister St. Peter had to be steered into a sitting position, with the greatest possible care, so as not to hurt her. Then her sleeves had to be turned up, again in a particular way; then I could take myself off. But I noticed before long the difficulty she had, with her poor crippled hands, about arranging the bread in her bowl; so that was another little thing to do before I left her. She hadn't asked me to do it, so she was greatly touched by having this attention paid to her; and it was this action (on which I'd bestowed no thought at all) that established me firmly in her favour. There was something even more important, though I only heard about it later; when I'd finished cutting her bread I gave her, before I left, my best smile. (Knox, *Autobiography*, pp. 295–297)

Pause: Reflect on how the pleasantness and graciousness of one or two particular people have helped you in times of difficulty.

THÉRÈSE'S WORDS

Of course, you don't meet enemies in Carmel; but when all is said and done you have your sympathies. One sister attracts you; another sister—well, you'd go a good long way round to avoid meeting her; without knowing it, she is your persecutress. Good; then Jesus tells me this is the sister I've got to love, the sister I've got to pray for. Her behaviour, to be sure, suggests that she isn't too fond of me. . . . (Knox, *Autobiography*, p. 271)

Here's a thing I've noticed—not that there's anything surprising about it. The holiest people in the community are the people one loves best; everybody is ready to talk to them, does them a good turn without being asked; in fact, it's exactly the people who could do without these attentions, without all this politeness, that are surrounded by marks of affection on every side. . . . On the other hand, people who suffer from imperfections get left out of things. Of course, one has to shew them all the politeness that is expected of religious, but, if only for fear of saying something unpleasant to them, one avoids their company.

When I describe such people as less than perfect, I'm not thinking only of spiritual imperfections; after all, the holiest of us won't actually be perfect till we get to heaven. I'm thinking of things like want of judgement, want of education, the touchiness you find in certain people's characters, which spoil the amenities of life. It's true, moral disabilities of this kind are chronic, there's no real hope of curing them. . . . What follows? Why, this: that at recreation, and at all time when freedom is granted us, I ought to single out the sisters who are least attractive to me, roadside casualties who need a good Samaritan. Often just a word or friendly smile are enough to make these difficult natures open out; but the charity I'm speaking of isn't practised merely with that end in view. It won't be long before I meet with discouragement; some remark of mine, quite innocently meant, will be taken up all wrong. But it isn't [a] waste of time, because my object in being kind to everybody, and especially to the less attractive ones, is to rejoice the heart of our Lord. (pp. 294–295)

REFLECTION

Thérèse felt antipathy toward some of the nuns and felt drawn toward others. But she accepted responsibility for those feelings without losing her inner freedom and without becoming victim to their dictates. She was aware of the feelings, but did not let them trap and overcome her. Rather, Thérèse challenged herself to be gracious and cheerful to those she was not attracted to.

🍂 Meditate on these questions; you may find that writing your reflections will be helpful.

- Who are the Sister Saint Peters in your life? In other words, which people in your day-to-day life are not always pleasant to be with, but need your help and graciousness?

  5: R·S; J·A·; C·P·

- Without denying any feelings of resistance you might have and without neglecting any of your duties, can you minister to these people in some way, if only with your graciousness?

Pray for the inner freedom and graciousness that you would need to be of assistance to these people.

🍂 Think of a recent situation that provoked strong feelings, hurt, and antipathy. Bring to mind the important details of the incident and all your feelings at the time. Speak to Jesus about the difficult situation and your feelings, and ask him to free you from being trapped by those emotions. Ask Jesus to fill you with the grace you need to respond with more freedom, generosity, and creativity.

🍂 In the form of a litany, thank God for people who, over the years, have borne your anger, foibles, inadequacies, illnesses, or emotional ups and downs. Offer God each name, ponder the graciousness of the person, and then say your words of thanks.

🐚 Reflect on the face that you present to other people. Do you offer people a cheerful and gracious presence? Is your smile mostly genuine or is it phony? To whom could you give the gift of your smile? Resolve to give this gift to someone who needs such quiet affirmation.

🐚 Spend time visiting or helping an elderly person or a primary caregiver.

🐚 Sit quietly and pray the gospel passage "From God's Word." For five or ten minutes, simply repeat these words slowly, allowing their truth to fill you.

FROM GOD'S WORD

[Jesus said:] "For if you love those who love you, what reward will you get? Do not even the tax collectors do as much? And if you save your greetings for your brothers, are you doing anything exceptional? Do not even the gentiles do as much? You must therefore set no bounds to your love. . . . In so far as you did this to one of the least of these brothers [and sisters] of mine, you did it to me." (Matthew 5:46-48; 25:40, NJB)

Closing prayer: Gracious God, give me the grace to understand and to practice what Thérèse speaks of when she says, "If charity is deep rooted in the soul, it shews up for all that" (Knox, *Autobiography*, p. 275).

MEDITATION ELEVEN

Zeal

Theme: Christian zeal for the good of other people finds expression in many ways. Thérèse reminds us that Christ effects the good and that cooperating with Christ will involve sharing in Christ's suffering.

Opening prayer: "Draw me into the furnace of [God's] love, to unite me ever more closely with himself, till it is he who lives and acts in me." (Knox, *Autobiography*, p. 310)

ABOUT THÉRÈSE

In her great concern that other people share in God's love and in her hope that her life would bear fruit for them, Thérèse held fast to three beliefs: that people in need would be liberated by experiencing God's love; that while she would cooperate through prayer and love, Jesus himself would actually do the good work; and that if she suffered to bring souls to God, she participated in the suffering of Christ.

Thérèse told this story about her zeal, even at age fourteen, for bringing people to God:

I'd been told about an abandoned wretch who'd just been condemned to death for his appalling crimes; and there was every reason to think that he would die impenitent. He must be saved from hell! I tried everything; there was nothing I could do myself, but I could offer to God our Lord's infinite merits, and all the treasury of his Church; and I would get Céline to have a Mass said for me. . . . In my heart, I felt certain we shouldn't be disappointed; but by way of encouragement in this practice of praying for sinners, I did ask for a sign. I told God I was sure he meant to pardon the unfortunate Pranzini, and I'd such confidence in our Lord's infinite mercy that I would cling to my belief even if Pranzini didn't go to confession, didn't make any gesture of repentance. Only I would like him to shew some sign of repentance, just for my own satisfaction.

My prayer was answered, and to the letter. . . . The day after his execution I came upon a copy of La Croix; . . . Pranzini didn't go to confession; he went up on to the scaffold, and was just preparing to put his head between the bars of the guillotine, when a sudden inspiration came to him. He availed himself of the crucifix which the priest was holding out to him, and kissed, three times, the sacred wounds. . . .

Well, there was my sign: and it fitted in exactly with the pattern of that grace which had moved me to pray for sinners. The thirst for souls had come to me upon sight of the precious blood flowing from our Lord's wounds. . . . (Knox, *Autobiography*, pp. 129–130)

Throughout her life, Thérèse felt called to help other people. She entered Carmel to save souls and to pray especially for priests. Later she volunteered to go as a missionary to the Carmelite convent in Saigon, Vietnam. On her deathbed she promised to spend eternity doing good on earth. Even though Thérèse never did leave her cloister at Lisieux, her zeal to save souls prompted Pope Pius XI to proclaim her patroness of the missions.

Pause: Ask God to bless today those who are poor and in bondage, oppressors and oppressed, those fighting hardness of heart, and all those who are not aware of God's love.

THÉRÈSE'S WORDS

Thérèse's zeal to cooperate in Christ's love for souls was particularly expressed in her willingness to identify with the suffering Jesus. A few weeks before she died, Thérèse said,

I tell God to apply all the prayers that are offered for me to sinners, and not to the relief of my pain. (O'Mahony, *Those Who Knew Her*, p. 270)

If I had been rich, I would have found it impossible to

see a poor person going hungry without giving him my possessions. And in the same way, when I gain any spiritual treasures, feeling that at this very moment there are souls in danger of being lost and falling into hell, I give them what I possess, and I have not yet found a moment when I can say: Now I'm going to work for myself. (Clarke, *Her Last Conversations*, p. 96)

On the last day of her life, in profound pain and distress, she said,
But God is not going to abandon me, I'm sure. . . . He has never abandoned me. . . . Never would I have believed it was possible to suffer so much! never! never! I cannot explain this except by the ardent desires I have had to save souls. (Clarke, *Her Last Conversations*, p. 205)

REFLECTION

"Zeal" may be a word that makes many of us uncomfortable. It sometimes smacks of a "do-good" attitude that turns people into projects. To call someone zealous frequently implies that they exude an overbearing and self-righteous fervor that overrides the sensibilities and integrity of other people. Thérèse meant something quite different.

Thérèse acknowledged that doing good without God's help is as impossible as making the sun shine at night. The fire of her zeal for bringing souls to Christ was kindled and fed by God's grace, not her own projects or ambition. Thérèse's zeal flowed from accepting God's love in her life, and God's love flowed through her in love and concern for other people. She wanted other people to experience God's love and liberating power for themselves.

❧ Slowly read the section "Thérèse's Words" again. Continue your meditation by reflecting on these questions:

- Would you describe yourself as being filled with zeal for bringing people to know God's love?

- Do you think of yourself as a person zealous to make your life fruitful for other people?

- Have you endured some privation or suffering to do good for someone?

- What elements of the good news set your heart on fire?

Talk to Jesus about your level of zeal; freely express your feelings. Ask Jesus to give you the grace that you need to let God's love flow through you.

Dorothy Day, co-founder of the Catholic Worker Movement and an admirer and biographer of Thérèse, noted that Thérèse, even as a child, was attracted to the corporal and spiritual works of mercy. Dorothy Day, whose cause for beatification is now being considered, also once remarked that doing the works of mercy was the only sure way of following the gospel.

As you review the corporal and spiritual works of mercy, examine the level of your zeal in performing these works. Rejoice over God's love flowing through you as you remember acting with mercy, and resolve to be open to God's grace in the future:

- Corporal Works: feeding the hungry, giving drink to the thirsty, clothing the naked, giving shelter to the homeless

- Spiritual Works: instructing the ignorant, counseling the doubtful, admonishing the sinner, bearing wrongs patiently, forgiving offenses, comforting the afflicted, praying for the living and the dead

Thérèse understood that by allowing herself to be drawn to Jesus she brought with her all those who had asked for prayers. She took to heart the passage from the Song of Songs that says: "Draw me in your footsteps, let us run" (1:4). Her prayer became the simple phrase "Draw me."

In rhythm with your breathing, quietly repeat the prayer, "Draw me," being confident that as you allow yourself to be drawn to God, all those who depend on you are also drawn to God.

❧ Several times during her life, Thérèse spoke of her hope to spend her heaven doing good on earth. Call upon Thérèse and discuss with her the good you need her to do in you, in your family, in the world.

FROM GOD'S WORD

[Jesus said:] "God, your Father, knows fully everything that you need. Don't worry. Instead, build the reign of God. Act with love. Everything else will be given you." (Adapted from Matthew 6:32–33)

Closing prayer: "Lord, . . . I'm such a poor thing—I haven't got it in me to give these children of yours their food. If you want each of them to get what she needs, you'll have to put it here, in my hand. . . . I'll simply pass on what you give me to each soul that comes to me for its food." (Knox, *Autobiography*, pp. 283–284)

Forgiving and Letting Go

Theme: No matter how difficult several troubled sisters made Thérèse's life, she readily forgave them and let go of any hurt and anger.

Opening prayer: "Dear Lord, you never tell us to do what is impossible, and yet you can see more clearly than I do how weak and imperfect I am; if, then, you tell me to love my sisters as you love them, that must mean that you yourself go on loving them in and through me." (Knox, *Autobiography*, p. 266)

ABOUT THÉRÈSE

When Thérèse entered the Carmelite cloister at Lisieux, she could not have known the problems that plagued the community, nor could she have been aware of the troubled personalities of some nuns with whom she was to live for the rest of her life. But not only did Thérèse treat the other nuns with graciousness, she learned to forgive and let go of her hurt.

Her older sister Pauline noticed this about Thérèse:

[She] sought the company of such [troubled] nuns in preference to that of others, and showed them the greatest kindness.

I considered the conduct of one of these to be particularly reprehensible, but Sister Thérèse insisted: "I assure you that I have the greatest compassion for Sister X. If you knew her as well as I do, you would see that she is not responsible for all of the things that seem so awful to us. I remind myself that if I had an infirmity such as hers, and so defective a spirit, I would not do any better than she does, and then I would despair; she suffers terribly from her own shortcomings." (O'Mahony, *Those Who Knew Her*, pp. 50–51)

Her sister Marie told one story of Thérèse's ability to love and to forgive those who were hard to like:

Her charity induced her to want to help a sister in the linen-room whose temperament was such that no one wanted to be in her company. This sister was subject to the blackest moods, and did scarcely any work. I saw her, when Sister Thérèse was already an invalid, come to her to call for the week's linen, which she had given [Thérèse] to repair, and because Sister Thérèse had not been able to complete her task, this sister reproached her severely instead of thanking her for what she had done in spite of being so ill. Sister Thérèse took the reproaches as if they were so much praise.

This poor, unfortunate sister became the object of Sister Thérèse's tenderest compassion. One day, when I had con-

Praying with Thérèse of Lisieux

fided to her how much trouble that sister gave me, [Sister Thérèse] said: "Ah! If you only knew how necessary it is to forgive her, how much she is to be pitied! It is not her fault if she is so poorly gifted; she is like an old clock that has to be re-wound every quarter of an hour. Yes, it is as bad as that. Well, wouldn't you have pity on it? Oh, how necessary it is to practice charity towards one's neighbour!" (O'Mahony, *Those Who Knew Her*, p. 94)

The following account was likely given by the same sister Thérèse forgave so much:

Sister Thérèse preferred to do good to those from whom she expected neither joy, nor comfort, nor tenderness. I was one of those. From the time I entered till she died I never felt any natural affection for her. I even avoided her. . . . I don't think I was ever a source of comfort to her. Still, she did not desert me, but showed me a lot of kindness. Whenever I was depressed she went out of her way to distract me and cheer me up. She never stopped trying to help me, but she was very discreet about it. When it was my turn to wash up, she often arranged things so that she could work beside me and chat to me. She showed trust in me, in an effort to enable me to trust her. . . . I've never seen her in bad humour, nor have I ever found her the slightest bit angry with me, even though her charitable advances were

128

not always returned in kind. . . . (O'Mahony, *Those Who Knew Her*, pp. 262–263)

Pause: Does anything prevent you from trying to understand and forgive the troublesome people in your life?

THÉRÈSE'S WORDS

Thérèse told the story of a relationship she had with one of the nuns she found very difficult to live with:

There's one sister in the community who has the knack of rubbing me up the wrong way at every turn; her tricks of manner, her tricks of speech, her character, just strike me as unlovable. But, then, she's a holy religious; God must love her dearly; so I wasn't going to let this natural antipathy get the better of me. I reminded myself that charity isn't a matter of fine sentiments; it means doing things. So I determined to treat this sister as if she were the person I loved best in the world. Every time I met her, I used to pray for her, offering to God all her virtues and her merits. I felt certain that Jesus would like me to do that, because all artists like to hear their work praised, and Jesus, who fashions men's souls so skilfully, doesn't want us to stand about admiring the façade—he wants us to make our way in, till we reach the inmost sanctuary which is his chosen dwelling, and admire the beauty of that. But I didn't confine myself to saying a lot of prayers for her, this sister who made life such a tug-of-war for me; I tried to do her every good turn I possibly could. When I felt tempted to take her down with an unkind retort, I would put on my best smile instead, and try to change the subject. . . . Once at recreation she actually said, beaming all over, something like this: "I wish you would tell me, Sister Thérèse of the Child Jesus, what it is about me that gets the right side of you? You've always got a smile for me whenever I see you." Well, of course, what really attracted me about her was Jesus hidden in the depths of her soul; Jesus makes the bitterest mouthful taste sweet. I could only say that the sight of her always made me smile with pleasure—naturally I didn't explain that the pleasure was entirely spiritual. (Knox, *Autobiography*, pp. 268–269)

In a further ironic twist to this story, Thérèse's sisters Céline and Marie thought that this nun was Thérèse's best friend in the convent.

REFLECTION

Many of the nuns Thérèse lived with during her nine years in Carmel assumed that charity came easily to her. Thérèse acted as if she liked everyone, even though she was deeply pained by some of the sisters. Only after Thérèse's death did most of the nuns become cognizant of the depth of Thérèse's courage and patience.

Thérèse knew that God was not asking her to confront or change the old and troubled nuns who disturbed her. Instead she tried to understand and forgive them. She experienced the feelings associated with having enemies, persons we find difficult, intimidating, or oppressive. But by loving those whom she found difficult, Thérèse returned good for evil. Part of her love consisted in trying to understand troublesome people; then, forgiving them; and finally, addressing their inner beauty instead of the troublesome behavior, letting go of any hurt or animosity and doing good.

☙ Thérèse dealt with some of the distressing behavior she encountered in others by trying to understand the sources of their distress. She tried to concentrate on the inner beauty of each person—the space in each of us where God dwells.

List three troublesome people in your life. Then ponder what you know about each person that might be a source of the distressing behavior. Ask God to help you see the presence of the Spirit in these people so that you can look beyond the disturbing aspects of their character. Finally, ask God for the grace to forgive the people on your list.

If you can come to a place of forgiveness toward any of these people, you may want to ritualize your forgiveness. For example, you might send a flower, anonymously, to someone who regularly acts in a way that irritates you. //

❧ The act of forgiving another person begins the process of healing our hurts, but the good news also calls us to let go of these hurts. On separate pieces of paper, briefly describe several hurtful memories, people, or situations that still bother you, make your blood boil, or pain you to remember. These should be situations over which you have no control and cannot change now.

Once you have written about each hurtful memory, read it carefully. Pray that God will help you let go of the resentment, anger, or hurt that still haunts you. Then let go of the memory through some ritual. For example, you might burn each piece of paper and, as the flames and smoke rise, pray, "Spirit of life, I let go of this pain. In its place, grant me new energy and joy." Or fold the pieces of paper into small boats that you release in a running stream.

❧ Select one person whose behavior bothers you. Day by day, try to consciously recall the presence of God in that person by some kind act. Smile and go out of your way to greet him or her. When you see the person, pray: "God, let me experience your presence through [name]."

FROM GOD'S WORD

[Jesus said:] "Love your enemies, do good to those who hate you, bless those who curse you, pray for those who treat you badly. To anyone who slaps you on one cheek, present the other cheek as well. . . .

". . . Do not judge, and you will not be judged; do not condemn, and you will not be condemned; forgive, and you will be forgiven." (Luke 6:27-29, 36-37, NJB)

Closing prayer: O my God, "I offer myself . . . to your merciful love, asking You to consume me incessantly, allowing the waves of infinite tenderness shut up within You to overflow into my soul, and that thus I may become a martyr of Your Love." (Clarke, *Story of a Soul*, p. 277)

Trusting God's Providence

Theme: Thérèse accepted all the experiences of her life as coming from God's providential care.

Opening prayer: "O my God, you have surpassed all I have hoped for, and I want to sing of your mercies." (Guy Gaucher, *The Story of a Life: St. Thérèse of Lisieux*, trans. Anne Marie Brennan, p. 140)

ABOUT THÉRÈSE

Thérèse knew of God's constant care from her own experience. As a child she had been alert to finding God's inspiration, especially in nature. A cluster of stars in the evening sky forming a T gave young Thérèse the idea that her "name was written in heaven," and she understood in a new way the limitations of "an ugly thing like the earth." At the age of five or six she visited the seashore: "I shall never forget the impression made on me by my first sight of the sea. I couldn't take my eyes off it, its vastness, the ceaseless roaring of the waves, spoke to me of the greatness and the power of God" (Knox, *Autobiography*, pp. 67, 74).

Thérèse identified herself with a flower, and in her memoirs, she wrote,

If a wild flower could talk, I imagine it would tell us quite
candidly about all God has done for it; there would be
no point in hushing up his gifts to it, out of mock humility, and pretending that it was ugly, that it had no smell,
that the sun had robbed it of its bloom, or the wind broken its stem, knowing that all that wasn't true. Anyhow,
this isn't going to be the *Autobiography* of a flower like
that. On the contrary, I'm delighted to be able to put them
on record, the favours our Lord has shown me, all quite
undeserved. I fully realise that there was nothing about me
which could have claimed his divine attention; anything
which is good in me is the effect of his mercy—that and
nothing else. (Knox, *Autobiography*, p. 36)

When Pauline was prioress in Carmel, she asked Thérèse to
write the memoirs of her early years. As Thérèse reminisced,
she saw clearly that God's mercy permeated all of her experiences. She recounted an incident showing her acceptance of all
of life as providential:

A day came when Léonie, thinking she was too old now
to play with dolls, came along to us with a basket full
of dresses and pretty little bits of stuff for making others, with her own doll lying on the top. "Here you are,
darlings," she said, "choose which of these you'd like;
they're all for you." . . . [I] said as I held out my hand:

"I choose the whole lot!" Then, without further ceremony, I took over the basket. . . .

Only a childish trait, perhaps, but in a sense it's been the key to my whole life. . . . There were plenty of degrees in spiritual advancement, and every soul was free to answer our Lord's invitation by doing a little for him, or by doing a lot for him; in fact, he gave it a choice between various kinds of self-sacrifice he wanted it to offer. And then, as in babyhood, I found myself crying out: "My God, I choose the whole lot. No point in becoming a Saint by halves. I'm not afraid of suffering for your sake; the only thing I'm afraid of is clinging to my own will. Take it, I want the whole lot, everything whatsoever that is your will for me." (Knox, *Autobiography*, pp. 51–52)

Pause: Do you believe that all the events in your life are guided by God and, therefore, that you can choose all of life because God is behind everything? (Status in C.M.)

THÉRÈSE'S WORDS

Thérèse was constantly aware of living in the palm of God's hand. She trusted that each experience, whether of joy or pain, was a merciful work of God. By reflecting on her life, she saw that God had been teaching her the ways of love and compassion:

It's an experience that makes me understand what's meant by the text, "The kingdom of God is here, within you." Our Lord doesn't need to make use of books or teachers in the instruction of souls; isn't he himself the Teacher of all teachers, conveying knowledge with never a word spoken? For myself, I never heard the sound of his voice, but I know that he dwells within me all the time, guiding me and inspiring me whenever I do or say anything. A light, of which I'd caught no glimmer before, comes to me at the very moment when it's needed; and this doesn't generally happen in the course of my prayer, however devout it may be, but more often in the middle of my daily work.

. . . Souls have got to fall into different groups, so that all God's perfections may be honoured severally. Only for me his infinite mercy is the quality that stands out in my life, and when I contemplate and adore his other perfections, it's against this background of mercy all the time. They all seem to have a dazzling outline of love; even God's justice, and perhaps his justice more than any other attribute of his, seems to have love for its setting. It's so wonderful to think that God is really just, that he takes all our weakness into consideration, that he knows our frail nature for what it is. What reason can I have for fear? . . .

How is it going to end, this story which I've called the story of a little white flower? . . . I can't tell. But I

> know that the mercy of God will always go with me. . . .
> (Knox, *Autobiography*, pp. 218–219, 221)

REFLECTION

Nothing extraordinary happened in Thérèse's life to manifest God's presence, but she believed that God loved her and guided her in all her experiences. It did not occur to her that physical, spiritual, or emotional pain signaled God's absence or anger. Because God's merciful providence permeates all of life, Thérèse knew that she did not need to manipulate events and people. God would provide. Thus she lived creatively, gratefully, and openly, alert to God's word in each experience, and accepting of God's love.

❧ Generally, we can cope with stress in one of three ways: we can change the situation that causes stress; we can move or get out of the stressful situation; or, we can change our attitude about the situation. Many times the third method of coping is the only one open to us.

List several stressful situations that you cannot change or move from but must cope with right now. Then ask God to show you how you might change your attitude about each situation so that you can see it as God's providing you with an opportunity to grow and learn. In solidarity with Thérèse, remind yourself that even through suffering, God's providence guides and protects us.

ॐ Our friends and family often most clearly manifest God's merciful providence. Compose and pray a litany of thanks for all the ways in which your family and friends mediate God's providential care for you. For instance, you might pray, "For Aunt Gertrude's willingness to babysit, thank you, gracious God," or "For Aimee's understanding when I was angry about work the other day, thank you, merciful God."

ॐ Repeat these words of Thérèse for several minutes in rhythm with your breathing and allow them to fill your heart: "I know that the mercy of God will always go with me."

ॐ Go for a walk or ride a bicycle. Look at, listen to, smell, and touch as much of what nature has to offer as you can.

If you cannot go outside, close your eyes and recall an experience in which the beauty and power of nature drew you out of yourself into the presence of God. Reflect on whatever enlightenment came to you at that time.

After your adventure in nature or in your memory, take a pen and a piece of paper and write your own psalm, expressing your thoughts and feelings about God's providential presence in nature.

❧ Be quiet in prayer for several moments. In rhythm with your breathing, repeat the prayer, "I want . . . everything . . . that is your will for me." As you inhale, become conscious of desiring to choose all that would please God; as you exhale, be conscious of desiring nothing that might block the actions of God in you.

❧ Sing your favorite hymn of thanksgiving for all of God's wonderful deeds in your life.

FROM GOD'S WORD

Your acts, O Yahweh, fill me with gladness;
I shout in triumph at your mighty deeds.
(Adapted from Psalm 92:4)

Closing prayer: "My God, I choose the whole lot. No point in becoming a Saint by halves. I'm not afraid of suffering for your sake; the only thing I'm afraid of is clinging to my own will. Take it, I want the whole lot, everything whatsoever that is your will for me." (Knox, *Autobiography*, pp. 51–52)

MEDITATION FOURTEEN
Living Truthfully

Theme: Thérèse sought to live truthfully, confident that God called her to be true to herself.

Opening prayer: "O my God, I really want to listen to You; I beg You to answer me when I say humbly: What is truth? Make me see things as they really are. Let nothing cause me to be deceived." (Clarke, *Her Last Conversations*, p. 105)

ABOUT THÉRÈSE

At the end of her life, Thérèse said, "I can nourish myself on nothing but the truth. . . . Yes, it seems to me I never sought anything but the truth . . . " (Clarke, *Her Last Conversations*, pp. 134, 205). For Thérèse, truth was a name for her beloved, Jesus. She sought personal union with the one who called himself "truth." She discovered truth in the deepest part of herself, in people, and in the ordinary events of life. In all her experiences, Thérèse strove for absolute honesty with herself and other people.

Thérèse's frankness, even as a small child, surprised her mother. "There she stands," her mother said, "always with the idea in her little head that she will be forgiven more readily if

---

141

she owns up. . . . At heart she's as good as gold, so loving and so open. You should see her running after me to tell me when she's been naughty. 'Mamma, I gave Céline a shove once, and I've slapped her once, but I'm not going to do it again.'" Her mother wrote to Pauline, describing four-year-old Thérèse: "She wouldn't tell a lie for all the money in the world" (Knox, *Autobiography*, pp. 41, 44, 53). This spirit of childhood honesty grew into Thérèse's profound sense of personal awareness and integrity.

Thérèse's acceptance of herself in the hands of the merciful God allowed her, without comparing herself with others, to rejoice in her weaknesses and blessings, because that simply was the truth. She freely admitted: "I'm resigned to seeing myself always far from perfect; even glad . . . " (Knox, *Autobiography*, p. 195).

In the same spirit of simple truth, Thérèse could also gratefully acknowledge God's gifts to her. For instance, she recounted this story about directing the novices:

The novices themselves can't understand it; they often ask me: "How do you manage to have an answer for everything?" . . . Some of them have such nice natures that they really believe I can read their hearts, just because I sometimes know what they're going to say before they've said it. One night, one of them had gone to bed in real anguish of mind, but she was determined to keep it dark from me; so she met me next morning with a smile on her face as she talked to me. And I, taking no notice of her remark, just said to her, as if I knew all about it: "Something is worrying you." She couldn't have been more surprised if I'd made the moon drop down at her feet. . . . I knew perfectly well that I hadn't the gift of reading people's hearts, and yet it had all fallen out so pat! Then of course I realised that God was there, at my elbow, and I'd simply used, like a child repeating its lesson, words that came from him, not from me. (Knox, *Autobiography*, pp. 290–291)

Pause: How is God calling you to become more and more true to yourself?

THÉRÈSE'S WORDS

In the opening pages of her memoirs, Thérèse noted that God calls all persons to accept the grace to be who they are:

But Jesus has been gracious enough to teach me a lesson about this mystery, simply by holding up to my eyes the book of nature. I realised, then, that all the flowers he has made are beautiful; the rose in its glory, the lily in its whiteness, don't rob the tiny violet of its sweet smell, or the daisy of its charming simplicity. I saw that if all these lesser blooms wanted to be roses instead, nature would lose the gaiety of her springtide dress—there would be no little flowers to make a pattern over the countryside. And so it is with the world of souls, which is his garden. He wanted to have great Saints, to be his lilies and roses, but he has made lesser Saints as well; and these lesser ones must be content to rank as daisies and violets, lying at his feet and giving pleasure to his eye like that. Perfection consists simply in doing his will, and being just what he wants us to be.

This, too, was made clear to me—that our Lord's love makes itself seen quite as much in the simplest of souls as in the most highly gifted, as long as there is no resistance offered to his grace. After all, the whole point of love is making yourself small; and if we were all like the great Doctors who have shed lustre on the Church by their brilliant teaching, there wouldn't be much condescension on God's part, would there, about coming into hearts like these? But no, he has created little children, who have no idea what's going on and can only express themselves by helpless crying: he has made the poor savages, with nothing better than the natural law to live by; and he is content to forget his dignity and come into their hearts too—these are the wild flowers that delight him by their simplicity. It is by such condescension that God shews his infinite greatness. The sun's light, that plays on the cedar-trees, plays on each tiny flower as if it were the only one in existence; and in the same way our Lord takes a special interest in each soul, as if there were no other like it. Everything conspires for the good of each individual soul, just as the march of the seasons is designed to make the most insignificant daisy unfold its petals on the day appointed for it. (Knox, *Autobiography*, pp. 34–35)

REFLECTION

Thérèse chose to be true to herself, despite her natural tendency to please other people. She saw herself as a little flower in God's garden and believed that if God made her that way, God wanted her that way. She did not uncritically appropriate the popular spiritual trends of the time or conform herself to some imposed model of holiness.

On one or two occasions, a spiritual director affirmed Thérèse's path, but her unique way of being with God was never really understood, even by those closest to her. Thérèse believed that Jesus alone was her spiritual director. She attended to her own inner lights and courageously trusted her own religious experience. Her path left her humanly lonely much of the time. In stark honesty, Thérèse's memoirs tell the story of her weaknesses and strengths, joys and sorrows, trials and consolations.

❧ Slowly read the section "Thérèse's Words" once or twice again. Picture all the flowers that she mentions. If any line strikes you as particularly important, stay with the line, letting its meaning become clear to you. Ask God to let the truth of Thérèse's words touch your heart.

❧ Imagine a garden filled with hundreds of varieties of flowers. This is God's garden. Which flower are you? Identify one flower that seems to harmonize with your image of your place in God's garden. What flower did you choose? What is it about this flower that makes it a symbol for you?

If you can find this flower at a florist's shop, in your yard, or in the country, buy or pick one and spend a few moments contemplating it. Each day thank God for the beauty of your flower. If you cannot buy or pick this flower, find a picture of it in a book and use it for your meditation.

❧ Reflect on Thérèse's insight that "perfection consists simply in doing his will, and being just what he wants us to be." Write out this phrase and post it where you will see it, especially in a place where you might be tempted to be too hard or too easy on yourself. Pray the words daily until they become part of your consciousness.

❧ Recall a circumstance in which you deceived yourself or violated your own truth and call. Bring to mind the time, place, situation, and persons involved. Remind yourself that Jesus, who is truth and knows what is in your heart, dwells with you. If he asked you each of these questions, how would you respond?

• What feelings urged you to deceive yourself?

• How did you feel during and after the deception?

• Are you in some pattern of self-deception about certain issues?

• What personal needs are you trying to meet when you deceive yourself in this way?

• What graces do you need to free yourself from self-deception?

Ask Jesus for the grace to be totally honest with yourself and to accept yourself in your weakness and strength.

☙ Thérèse experienced God's presence in truth and in love. For her, truth and love were inseparable. Meditatively pray the phrase "Truth and Love." Allow the awareness of God's presence to grow in you.

✤ Thérèse believed that everything works out for the good of each person. In the face of the power of evil in our lives, this idea may seem naive. But try to remember an event in your own life that at first seemed to be of no good, yet later became an experience of grace. Talk to Jesus about the transforming gift of this seemingly bad event.

FROM GOD'S WORD

Yahweh is merciful and forgiving,
slow to anger, rich in love.
(Adapted from Psalm 103:8)

Closing prayer: Join Thérèse in her prayer: "[Our Lord], who cried out in his mortal life, 'Father, I give thee praise that thou hast hidden all this from the wise and the prudent, and revealed it to little children.' And now, just because I was so helpless and insignificant, he saw in me the opportunity for a startling exercise of his mercy. He brought himself down to my level, and taught me, all unobserved, the lesson of love." (Knox, *Autobiography*, p. 136)

MEDITATION FIFTEEN

Grace in Desolation

Theme: Thérèse's spiritual journey, which began with childlike consolations and intimacy with God, ended with profound spiritual desolation. On her deathbed, she identified herself with those who had lost all faith, but still she clung to God.

Opening prayer: "In the evening of this life, I shall appear before You with empty hands, for I do not ask You, Lord, to count my works. All our justice is stained in Your eyes. I wish, then, to be clothed in Your own Justice and to receive from Your Love the eternal possession of Yourself. I want no other Throne, no other Crown but You, my Beloved." (Clarke, *Story of a Soul*, p. 277)

ABOUT THÉRÈSE

During the last eighteen months of her life, Thérèse experienced acute physical pain and total spiritual desolation. In her body, she suffered the torment of tuberculosis that had even spread to her intestines. In her heart, she suffered a complete loss of faith. Thérèse was plunged into such spiritual darkness that she spoke of being capable of blasphemy.

To all appearances, Thérèse seemed to be suffering very little, so constant was her cheerfulness during the last months. Her kindness cloaked severe irritation at one or two of the nuns who disturbed her by inopportune visits, frivolous questions, constant staring, and indiscreet laughter that sometimes seemed to be jeering. Finally, her physical distress and spiritual weariness became so intense that she warned her sisters not to leave anything poisonous nearby: "If I had not had any faith, I would have committed suicide without an instant's hesitation" (Clarke, *Her Last Conversations*, p. 196).

Despite the care and loving attention given by her blood sisters and other nuns, Thérèse suffered her inner trials alone. Ironically, her sisters added to her difficulty by attempting to console her. They wanted Thérèse to die in a manner that would confirm their belief in her sanctity, fulfilling the blissful descriptions of death hinted at by saints like Teresa of Ávila. In addition, the nuns desired that she predict the day of her death and die on a special feast day after receiving the last sacraments.

At this point in her life, to die like a saint seemed completely irrelevant to Thérèse. In response to her sisters' statement that she was a saint, Thérèse responded: "No . . . I'm a very little soul upon whom God has bestowed graces; that's what I am" (Clarke, *Her Last Conversations*, p. 143). She was not concerned about a "good" or "happy" death, as current piety then interpreted the phrase: "If some morning you find me dead, you must not be unhappy about that, for then God has simply come for me. Undoubtedly it is a great grace to receive the Sacraments, but if God does not permit it, that is well, too. . . . All is grace" (Görres, *The Hidden Face*, p. 378).

Pause: Reflect on Thérèse's favorite passage from Job: "Even if God were to kill me, I would continue to hope in God" (adapted from 13:15).

THÉRÈSE'S WORDS

I couldn't believe that there really were godless people who had no faith at all; it was only by being false to his own inner convictions that a man could deny the existence of heaven. . . .

But there are souls which haven't got any faith. . . . And now, in those happy days of Easter-tide, Jesus taught me to realise that. He allowed my soul to be overrun by an impenetrable darkness which made the thought of heaven, hitherto so welcome, a subject of nothing but conflict and torment. And this trial was not to be a matter of a few days or a few weeks; it was to last until the moment when God should see fit to remove it. And that moment hasn't come yet.

I wish I could put down what I feel about it, but unfortunately that isn't possible; to appreciate the darkness of this tunnel, you have to have been through it. Perhaps, though, I might try to explain it by a comparison. You must imagine that I've been born in a country entirely overspread with a thick mist. . . .

. . . And now, all of a sudden, the mists around me have become denser than ever; they sink deep into my soul and wrap it round so that I can't recover the dear image of my native country any more—everything has disappeared.

I get tired of the darkness all around me, and try to refresh my jaded spirits with the thoughts of that bright country where my hopes lie; and what happens? It is worse torment than ever; the darkness itself seems to borrow, from the sinners who live in it, the gift of speech. I hear its mocking accents: "It's all a dream, this talk of a heavenly country, bathed in light, scented with delicious perfumes, and of a God who made it all, who is to be your possession in eternity! You really believe, do you, that the mist which hangs about you will clear away later on? All right, all right, go on longing for death! But death will make nonsense of your hopes; it will only mean a night darker than ever, the night of mere nonexistence."

. . . But how can I go on writing about it without running the risk of talking blasphemously? . . . If I've done Jesus an injury, may he forgive me for it; he knows well enough that I do try to live the faith, even when I get no satisfaction out of it. . . .

. . . To judge by the sentiments I express in all the nice little poems I've made up during the last year, you might imagine that my soul was as full of consolations as it could hold; that, for me, the veil of faith which hides the unseen scarcely existed. And all the time it isn't just a veil, it's a great wall which reaches up to the sky and blots out the stars! (Knox, *Autobiography*, pp. 253–257)

After months of desolation, the last entry Thérèse made in her memoirs spoke words of confidence.

I'm certain of this—that if my conscience were burdened with all the sins it's possible to commit, I would still go and throw myself into our Lord's arms, my heart all broken up with contrition; I know what tenderness he has for any prodigal child of his that comes back to him. (Knox, *Autobiography*, p. 312)

And three weeks before she died Thérèse said,

I'm like a tired and harassed traveller, who reaches the end of his journey and falls over. Yes, but I'll be falling into God's arms!." (Clarke, *Her Last Conversations*, p. 191)

REFLECTION

When Pius XI canonized Thérèse, he stressed that she was specifically significant for our own time because she fulfilled her vocation "without leaving the common order of things." . . . She is the saint of the "common order of things" precisely because she represented a total love of God and a total belief in God in the very predicament where most people find themselves, namely sin and unbelief. . . . Unlike so many exponents of the ways of piety, she neither bullies us nor teases us from any position of elevation; she simply gets on with loving God as one of us. And in so doing she shows us that precisely as sinners, as doubters, we are welcome to run to God's love. Her acceptance of darkness identifies our darkness as a thirst for God, and at the same time assures us that even in this very darkness Christ is there thirsting for our love. (Tugwell, *Ways of Imperfection*, p. 229)

To those who are fearful and find trust and love difficult, Thérèse would say that there is no need to be discouraged. Rather, let fear and doubt be an experience of the weakness that God will transform in the flames of love.

❧ Remember a time in your life when you were filled with fear and doubt about God. Ponder the truth that sinners, doubters, and persons filled with fear are the most welcome to God's love. Ask God to help you value the darkness, because in the darkness we experience a thirst for God. Share with God a specific concern you have that is hidden in one of those dark places of your heart.

❧ Write a prayer of thanksgiving for the people who give you hope in times of desolation, people who give you patience and confidence to not "give up" on God or on yourself.

❧ Sit quietly and make "All is Grace" your prayer word. Recite it slowly and reverently.

❧ Thérèse imaged herself dying like a tired traveler coming to the end of a journey and falling over: "Yes, but I'll be falling into God's arms." Imagine yourself falling into God's arms. What thoughts and feelings come to you? Share with God your sentiments and ask Thérèse to intercede for you for an increase in the spirit of total trust in God.

FROM GOD'S WORD

Yahweh, you are my shepherd;
I shall not want.
In verdant pastures you give me repose.
Beside restful waters you lead me;
you refresh my soul.
You guide me in right paths
for your name's sake.
Even though I walk in the dark valley
I fear no evil;
for you are at my side.
(Adapted from Psalm 23:1-4)

Closing prayer: "Lord, have mercy on us, we are sinners! Send us home restored to your favour. May all those who have no torch of faith to guide them catch sight, at least, of its rays. . . . All I ask is that no sin of mine may offend you." (Knox, *Autobiography*, pp. 254–255)

"Perfection consists in doing his will, and being just what he wants us to be."
(St. Thérèse)

For Further Reading

Clarke, John, trans. *St. Thérèse of Lisieux: Her Last Conversations*. Washington, DC: ICS Publications, 1977.

Clarke, John, trans. *Story of a Soul:The Autobiography of St. Thérèse of Lisieux*. Washington, DC: ICS Publications, 1975.

Gaucher, Guy. *The Story of a Life: St. Thérèse of Lisieux*. Trans. Anne Marie Brennan. New York: Harper & Row, 1987.

Görres, Ida Friederike. *The Hidden Face: A Study of St. Thérèse of Lisieux*. Trans. Richard and Clara Winston. New York: Pantheon, 1959.

Jamart, François. *Complete Spiritual Doctrine of St. Thérèse of Lisieux*. Trans. Walter Van De Putte. New York: Alba House, 1961.

Knox, Ronald, trans. *Autobiography of St. Thérèse of Lisieux*. New York: P. J. Kenedy and Sons, 1958.

O'Mahony, Christopher, ed. and trans. *St. Thérèse of Lisieux by Those Who Knew Her*. Huntington, IN: Our Sunday Visitor, 1975.

Sullivan, John, ed. *Experiencing St. Thérèse Today*. Washington, DC: ICS Publications, 1990.

Thérèse, of Lisieux, Saint. *General Correspondence*, vols. 1 and 2. Trans. John Clarke. Washington, DC: ICS Publications, 1982 and 1988.

Tugwell, Simon. *Ways of Imperfection: An Exploration of Christian Spirituality*. Springfield, IL: Templegate Publishers, 1985.

Acknowledgments

The scriptural material found on pages 101, 109, 125, 140, 148, and 155 is freely adapted. These adaptations are not to be understood or used as official translations of the Bible.

All other scriptural quotations used in this book are from the New Jerusalem Bible. Copyright © 1985 by Darton, Longman & Todd, London, and Doubleday, a division of Random House, Inc. Used with permission.

Selections from the *Complete Spiritual Doctrine of St. Thérèse of Lisieux*, by Rev. Francois Jamart, translated by Rev. Walter Van De Putte (New York: Alba House, 1961), Copyright © 1961 by Society of St. Paul.

Selections from *Saint Thérèse of Lisieux: General Correspondence*, vol. 1, translated by John Clarke, OCD (Washington, DC: ICS Publications, 1982), Copyright © 1982 by the Washington Province of Discalced Carmelite Friars, ICS Publications, 2131 Lincoln Road NE, Washington, DC 20002 USA. Used with permission.

Selections from the *Autobiography of St. Thérèse of Lisieux*, translated by Ronald Knox (New York: P. J. Kenedy & Sons, 1958), Copyright © 1958 by P. J. Kenedy & Sons; copyright renewed. Reprinted with the permission of Macmillan Publishing Company.

Selections from *St. Thérèse of Lisieux: Her Last Conversations*, translated by John Clarke, OCD (Washington, DC: ICS Publications, 1977), Copyright © 1977 by the Washington Province of Discalced Carmelites, ICS Publications, 2131 Lincoln Road NE, Washington, DC 20002 USA. Used with permission.

Selections from *Story of a Soul: The Autobiography of St. Thérèse of Lisieux*, translated by John Clarke, OCD (Washington, DC: ICS Publications, 1975), Copyright © 1975, 1976 by the Washington Province of Discalced Carmelites, ICS Publications, 2131 Lincoln Road NE, Washington, DC 20002 USA. Used with permission.

Selections from *Saint Thérèse of Lisieux: General Correspondence*, vol. 2, translated by John Clarke, OCD (Washington, DC: ICS

Publications, 1988), Copyright © 1988 by the Washington Province of Discalced Carmelite Friars, ICS Publications, 2131 Lincoln Road NE, Washington, DC 20002 USA. Used with permission.

Selections from *The Hidden Face: A Study of St. Thérèse of Lisieux*, by Ida Friederike Görres, translated by Richard and Clara Winston (New York: Pantheon, 1959), Copyright © 1959 by Ida Friederike Görres. Used by permission of Random House.

Selections from *Ways of Imperfection: An Exploration of Christian Spirituality*, by Simon Tugwell (Springfield, IL: Templegate Publishers, 1985), Copyright © 1985 by Simon Tugwell and Darton, Longman & Todd, London. Used by permission of the publishers.

Selections from *St. Thérèse of Lisieux by Those Who Knew Her*, edited and translated by Christopher O'Mahony (Huntington, IN: Our Sunday Visitor, 1975), Copyright © 1975 by Christopher O'Mahony. First published by Veritas Publications. Used with permission of Veritas Publications.

Selections from Carmelite Studies V: *Experiencing St. Thérèse Today*, edited by John Sullivan, OCD (Washington, DC: ICS Publications, 1990), Copyright © 1990 by the Washington Province of Discalced Carmelite Friars, ICS Publications, 2131 Lincoln Road NE, Washington, DC 20002 USA. Used with permission.

Selections from *The Story of a Life: St. Thérèse of Lisieux*, by Guy Gaucher, translated by Anne Marie Brennan (New York: Harper & Row, Publishers, 1987), Copyright © 1987 by Harper & Row, Publishers.

the WORD
among us ®
The *Spirit* of Catholic Living

This book was published by The Word Among Us. Since 1981, The Word Among Us has been answering the call of the Second Vatican Council to help Catholic laypeople encounter Christ in the Scriptures.

The name of our company comes from the prologue to the Gospel of John and reflects the vision and purpose of all of our publications: to be an instrument of the Spirit, whose desire is to manifest Jesus' presence in and to the children of God. In this way, we hope to contribute to the Church's ongoing mission of proclaiming the gospel to the world so that all people would know the love and mercy of our Lord and grow ever more deeply in love with him.

Our monthly devotional magazine, *The Word Among Us*, features meditations on the daily and Sunday Mass readings, and currently reaches more than one million Catholics in North America and another half million Catholics in one hundred countries around the world. Our book division, The Word Among Us Press, publishes numerous books, Bible studies, and pamphlets that help Catholics grow in their faith.

To learn more about who we are and what we publish, log on to our website at www.wau.org. There you will find a variety of Catholic resources that will help you grow in your faith.

Embrace His Word, Listen to God . . .

www.wau.org